Contents

1 Sources of law

Common law and equity

Development of the common law

Before the Norman Conquest, there was no unified system of law.

Types of courts

The Norman Conquest

Generally, law is regarded as beginning with the Norman Conquest, which made many changes. There was a strong centralised government headed by the King and advised by his Council (*Curia Regis*).

The common law

A common law was established by the 'general eyre', which eventually created the first national courts. Good local customs were applied promoting certainty and consistency; the doctrine of *stare decisis* ('the decision stands') was born.

Defects of the common law: rise of equity

Writs were very specific. In common law, if there was no writ, there was no remedy. Money damages were the only remedy. The law favoured the rich and many rights were not recognised. No right of subpoena existed to compel witnesses to give evidence.

The rise of equity
Equity created new rights. New procedures were introduced, for example, the right to subpoena and discovery of documents. The rich nobles resented equity because of the reduction in their incomes. This resulted in the Provisions of Oxford 1258, prohibiting expansion of writs. This statute was later modified after complaints.

Equitable remedies

injunction → specific performance

rescission → rectification

Advantages of equity
Equity was less rigid and formal than the common law, resulting in more flexibility. It was fairer, dealing with cases on their merit. It was described as a 'gloss upon the law'.

Defects of equity
Equity lacked certainty. It varied from chancellor to chancellor. It became overburdened and slow moving.

The Judicature Acts 1873–75
The Judicature Acts resolved the difficulties and reorganised the existing courts, fusing the common law courts and the court of chancery. Both common law and equity decisions could be given in any court.

European Community law

As a result of the European Communities Act 1972, the UK and its citizens are subject to European Community law. The Community is part of a wider legal institution, the European Union.

uropean institutions

Sources of Community law

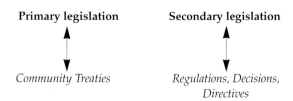

Primary legislation   **Secondary legislation**

↑   ↑
↓   ↓

Community Treaties   *Regulations, Decisions,*
                                          Directives

Community law has a higher legal status than domestic law. In *Factortame Ltd v Secretary of State for Transport (No 2)* (1991), the House of Lords considered the relationship between UK and Community law. It confirmed that the effect of the European Communities Act 1972 was that Community law has supremacy over all UK law (in this case, the Merchant Shipping Act 1988), even in the face of Parliament's express intention to contradict Community law. This case has significant constitutional importance, since it suggests that the Parliament of 1972 was able to bind the Parliament of 1988, going against traditional notions of parliamentary sovereignty. Parliament, though, still retains the right to repeal the 1972 Act and, therefore, to leave the jurisdiction of the European Union.

European Convention on Human Rights

The Convention is signed by the 43 members of the Council of Europe. It protects the fundamental rights and freedoms of all members of the signatory States.

Institutions

| European Commission of Human Rights | — | European Court of Human Rights (in Strasbourg) |

Human Rights Act 1998

On 2 October 2000, the Human Rights Act 1998 came into force, incorporating key parts of the Convention into UK law. All public bodies now have a duty to act in accordance with the Convention, and those who have their rights infringed have a remedy in the domestic courts. Also, the courts must construe all legislation, so far as possible, in a way which is compatible with the Convention. If it is impossible to do so, a declaration of incompatibility must be made. The impact of the Act is already proving to be significant and wide-ranging.

Domestic law

The legislative procedure

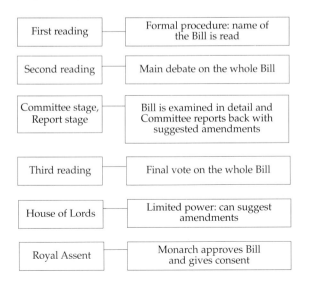

First reading	Formal procedure: name of the Bill is read
Second reading	Main debate on the whole Bill
Committee stage, Report stage	Bill is examined in detail and Committee reports back with suggested amendments
Third reading	Final vote on the whole Bill
House of Lords	Limited power: can suggest amendments
Royal Assent	Monarch approves Bill and gives consent

Acts of Parliament

Delegated legislation

Promulgated by bodies other than Parliament itself, this type of legislation is necessary for expediency. It is sometimes known as subordinate legislation, but is not inferior to other legislation.

Orders in Council

Statutory instruments

Byelaws

Advantages and disadvantages of delegated legislation

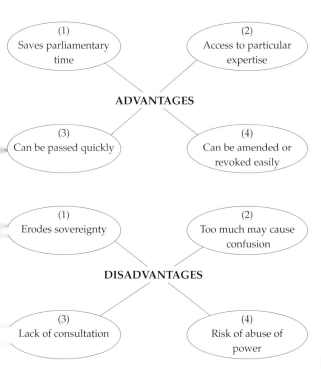

ADVANTAGES

(1) Saves parliamentary time

(2) Access to particular expertise

(3) Can be passed quickly

(4) Can be amended or revoked easily

DISADVANTAGES

(1) Erodes sovereignty

(2) Too much may cause confusion

(3) Lack of consultation

(4) Risk of abuse of power

Case law

Created by judges when interpreting statutes or the common law, case law is criticised for its inconsistency and bulk; it is preponderous in nature. Difficulties can arise when determining the law in a particular judgment. However, case law is flexible and can reflect current changes in society.

2 The legal profession

Barristers: training and nature of the work

Barristers are known as the court advocates and consultant specialists of the legal profession.

Barristers' training

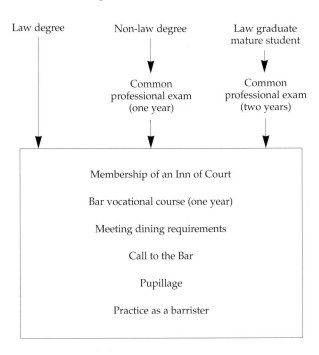

Law degree

Non-law degree → Common professional exam (one year)

Law graduate mature student → Common professional exam (two years)

Membership of an Inn of Court

Bar vocational course (one year)

Meeting dining requirements

Call to the Bar

Pupillage

Practice as a barrister

Nature of the work

Barristers generally work in chambers, although it is no longer compulsory for them to do so. They are now permitted to practise alone, working from an office or home. Working from the Bar Library is now no longer necessary. The rule that barristers must deal with clients directly has been modified so that accountants and other professionals can instruct a barrister. Barristers are now allowed to advertise their services in newspapers, a major change introduced under the Courts and Legal Services Act 1990.

Advocates' liability

The House of Lords recently held, in *Arthur JS Hall and Co v Simons* (2000), that it is no longer in the public interest for advocates to have immunity from suit. Barristers can now, therefore, be sued for professional negligence alleged to have occurred in court (barristers would previously be sued for alleged out-of-court preparatory work).

Conduct of barristers

The Bar is regulated by a Code of Conduct. One of the main provisions of the Code is the 'cab rank' rule. Barristers are duty bound to accept any case that comes to them, if they have the time and expertise to do it. Barristers are also not allowed to discriminate in respect of the type of clients they will represent, so that access to the barrister is open to all, regardless of sex, race, etc.

Bar statistics

According to the latest figures (General Council of the Bar, 1 October 2000), there are 10,132 barristers in independent practice in England and Wales, of whom 7,494 are men and 2,638 are women. 784 of all barristers are from an ethnic minority background, of whom 301 are women. Of the 783 pupils in 2000–01, 376 were women and 139 were from an ethnic minority background.

Solicitors: training and nature of the work

Solicitors' training

Nature of the work

The work of a solicitor is very varied. They advise and represent clients, draw up wills, contracts and partnership agreements, do conveyancing, matrimonial work, form companies and deal with accident claims, etc. They are responsible for all the preparatory pre-court work. They are entitled to rights of audience in lower courts and in uncontested cases in the High Court. They can also now gain rights of audience in the higher courts. The details and implications of this are discussed later in this chapter.

Legal executives: role and training

The Institute of Legal Executives

The Institute of Legal Executives (ILEX) was established in 1963 and is the governing body for legal executives. The Institute provides training and a career structure for solicitors' staff. Legal executives play an important role and can be involved in specialised areas, such as probate, trust work, conveyancing, matrimonial, civil or criminal litigation. Employed by solicitors, they can deal comprehensively with the client and manage branch offices. They have no rights of audience, but can appear in front of a judge on uncontested matters.

Training

There is a two part training scheme. Part I involves a broad introduction to key areas of law. In Part II, students study four subjects in more depth. To qualify as a Fellow, a member must be 25 and have a minimum of five years' experience in legal practice.

The changing legal profession

Although the Benson Commission on Legal Services (1979) unanimously rejected the idea of fusing the two branches of the profession, changes in the law have meant that there is less and less distinction between solicitors' and barristers' work. Solicitors' monopolies over conveyancing and the right to conduct litigation have been technically removed (by the Courts and Legal Services Act (CLSA) 1990 and the Access to Justice Act 1999 respectively) and the Bar's monopoly over rights of audience, even in the higher courts, has also been removed. Barristers can also now be employed as in-house lawyers.

Other professional bodies

Other professional bodies can now offer legal services, the intention being to increase competition and improve the legal services being offered to the public in terms of quality and price. The Administration of Justice Act 1985 ended solicitors' monopoly on conveyancing, allowing licensed conveyancers to practice in this area. Non-lawyers can also apply to have rights of audience in the courts.

The Courts and Legal Services Act 1990

The government's overall objective in introducing this legislation was:

> ... to see that the public has the best possible access to legal services and that those services are of the right quality for the particular needs of the client.

The main changes that the Act made are:

- the establishment of the Lord Chancellor's Advisory Committee on Education and Conduct;

- the establishment of the Legal Services Ombudsman;

- the extension of rights of audience, rights to conduct litigation and undertake probate work to suitably qualified persons, even to non-lawyers;

- new regulations and codes setting qualification standards and practice requirements for advocacy and litigation;

- ending restrictions on multi-disciplinary and multi-national partnerships (although barristers are still restricted by the Bar Code of Conduct);

- changes in the rules of eligibility for judicial appointment to reflect the enjoyment of advocacy rights rather than status as barrister or solicitor.

Section 17 governs the regulation of non-lawyers, setting out the guidelines for granting rights of audience. Solicitors who wish to gain the higher courts qualification must show two years' experience of advocacy in the lower courts and experience of the procedures of the relevant higher court, competency in a written test on evidence and procedure, and satisfactory completion of an advocacy training course. Figures show there has been a steady increase in the number of solicitor-advocates, now totalling over 1,000. There is considerable anxiety amongst barristers that solicitors will gradually take much of the work from the Bar. Although barristers will remain the advocacy specialists of the profession, they are up against solicitors who can afford to charge less. Some barristers fear that the result of this legislation will be a gradual deterioration of the standard of advocacy in our courts. It has been argued on the other hand that the increase in competition can only increase standards.

Another new development is BarDirect, a scheme set up in 1999 that enables certain professions and organisations to have direct access to barristers without going through a solicitor. It is not yet known how much of an impact this will have on the legal profession, but it is suspected that it will mostly be used by a few specific organisations (for example, police forces, trades unions, doctors' defence bodies) who require a specialised opinion, and hence its effect will be limited.

Access to Justice Act 1999

The Access to Justice Act 1999 extends the principle that all lawyers should enjoy full rights of audience. It provides that every barrister and every solicitor has a right of audience before every court in relation to all proceedings. The only remaining restriction on this right is the obligation to meet training requirements that may be prescribed, and to obey the rules of conduct of the professional body. The Act also makes it clear that the overriding duties of all advocates and litigators are their duty to the court to act with independence and in the interests of justice, and their duty to comply with their professional bodies' rules of conduct.

The Act also simplifies and speeds up the procedure for authorising further professional bodies to grant rights of audience to its members, signalling a widening of those rights in the future.

The Legal Services Ombudsman

This position was created by the CLSA 1990 to investigate allegations relating to the way in which a complaint made to a professional body with respect to legal services has been dealt with.

3 The judiciary

The judiciary consists of 5 heads of division, 12 Lords of Appeal in Ordinary (Law Lords), 35 Lords Justice of Appeal, 107 High Court judges, 616 circuit judges, 1,329 Recorders and 403 district judges.

Appointment and tenure

The Act of Settlement 1700 laid down the statutory foundation for the appointment of judges. Judges held office *quamdiu se bene gesserint* (if they were of good behaviour). This gave judges security of tenure and they could be removed only upon address of both Houses of Parliament. However, no English judge has been removed under this procedure. This security of tenure available to the superior judge is not enjoyed by circuit judges or recorders; they can be removed by the Lord Chancellor for misbehaviour or incapacity. From April 1995, posts for circuit judges and district judges must be advertised, applicants being selected by a panel. This move was intended to combat some of the criticisms in respect of the appointment of judges.

The independence of the judiciary

Judges must be completely impartial when applying the law and should not allow any political favour or bias to influence their judgment. The idea of the independence of the judiciary from the State is important to the legal system; protection from removal and the doctrine of judicial immunity reinforces this. Much stress is laid upon the constitutional importance of the independence of judges and accords with Montesquieu's theory of the separation of the powers. To maintain the idea of non-political interference, judges cannot be members of Parliament. However, the Lord Chancellor's position is rather incongruous, having a foot in both camps – being a political appointee and member of the government.

Judicial immunity from civil suit protects superior judges in respect of their activities during the course of judicial office.

Judicial offices

The Lord High Chancellor

↓

Lord Chief Justice

↓

Master of the Rolls

↓

Vice Chancellor

↓

President of the Family Division

↓

Lords of Appeal in Ordinary

↓

Lord Justices of Appeal

↓

High Court judges

↓

Circuit judges

↓

District judges

Social background of the judiciary

The judiciary is criticised because its members are usually drawn from a very elite social background, mostly from public schools and Oxford or Cambridge universities. They are from upper middle class origins and it is suggested that, because of this and their isolation from life within society, they are out of touch with the moral values of the generation they are trying and sentencing.

Training of judges

Judges receive training from the Judicial Studies Board (JSB). According to the Annual Report for 2000–01, 3,613 judges and part time judges and 67 tribunal members participated in the Human Rights Act programme, the largest ever undertaken by the Board. In June 2000, the Board ratified a three-year Equal Treatment strategy, the main aim of which is to see the full integration of equal treatment issues in all of the JSB's core training courses.

Magistrates

Lay justices

Lay justices sit in magistrates' courts, are part time and are unpaid, receiving only expenses. They try the majority of minor criminal offences; approximately 98% of all criminal offences are processed through the magistrates' court. Lay justices are vital to the legal system as they provide a cheap and quick system of justice. They are appointed by the Lord Chancellor from individuals put forward by local organisations. They must be over 21, not be over 70 and, usually, must live or work in the particular area.

Unlike superior judges, magistrates are not subject to the doctrine of judicial independence; many are local councillors. Though a balance is attempted to ensure that certain groups in the population are represented, many groups are, in fact, excluded. Magistrates are predominantly white, middle class males and this imbalance causes concern. There are not enough women magistrates: research by Baldwin (1976) showed this tendency to be prevalent and the feeling is that magistrates are not a true representation of the community.

District judges (magistrates' court)
The Access to Justice Act 1999 introduced the name 'district judge (magistrates' court)' to replace 'stipendiary magistrate', and re-organised all such judges into a single 'bench'. District judges are paid, and are usually barristers or solicitors. They preside over busy magistrates' courts where the use of lay justices would be impracticable; they can sit on their own.

The justices' clerk
Lay magistrates can only sit if they have a qualified clerk to assist them. He advises the justices as to the law and practice; however, he is not allowed to interfere with their decision. The clerk is salaried, and is usually a barrister or solicitor.

Judicial reasoning

Case law and judicial precedent
A prominent element of common law systems is the principle of *stare decisis*. It is common to speak today of law being 'judge made'. When deciding a case, judges must look to previous case law decided in similar cases. Judges are bound to decide cases using existing legal principles. The doctrine of judicial precedent depends on the hierarchy of the courts for its operation; courts are bound to follow decisions of higher courts and, usually, previous decisions of its own.

Hierarchy of English courts

Court	Courts bound by it	Courts it must follow
European Court	The court which made the preliminary reference	None
House of Lords	All English courts	None
Court of Appeal	Divisional courts High Court Crown Courts County courts Magistrates' courts	House of Lords
Divisional courts	High Court Crown Courts County courts Magistrates' courts	House of Lords Court of Appeal
High Court	County courts Magistrates' courts	House of Lords Court of Appeal Divisional courts
Crown Courts County courts Magistrates' courts	None	House of Lords Court of Appeal Divisional courts High Court

The House of Lords

Since 1966, the House is no longer bound by its own decisions. All decisions of the House of Lords are binding on all other courts.

Statutory interpretation

It is not an easy task for courts to interpret Acts of Parliament. Problems of construction arise when judges have to use their traditional skills to resolve them. There is no Act of Parliament to guide judges in the interpretation of other Acts, although the Interpretation Act 1978 gives some assistance. Judges can refer to the explanations when

Three main rules

The Mischief Rule	The Golden Rule
Rule in *Heydon's Case* (1584). The courts look to the purpose of the Act to fulfil that purpose	Supplements the literal rule. Words should be interpreted to give best effect to Parliament's intention

The Literal Rule
Simple words which have obvious everyday meanings should be given that meaning by the court

Maxims of interpretation

Ejusdem generis	*Expressio unius exclusio alterus*	*Noscitur a sociis*
Categories of words and classes of persons are referred to only if they are in the classification	This will exclude other members if a specific member of a class is mentioned	Must read words in the section in this context

dealing with issues of EC law. As more laws become statute based, interpretation of these statutes is a key role of a judge.

Since the decision in *Pepper v Hart* (1993), a judge can refer to parliamentary debates (*Hansard*) to aid him in interpretation of a statute. However, the rule has its limitations: it can only be used if the statute is ambiguous or if the use of the literal meaning would lead to an absurdity.

Rules of statutory construction
When statutory words are ambiguous, judges can use rules of construction to aid them in determining what it was Parliament had intended.

Intrinsic aids

The title (long or short)	Preamble	Headings

Interpreting EC law
The Treaty of Rome (the EC Treaty) confers exclusive jurisdiction on the ECJ to interpret EC law. When a question of EC law is raised in the English courts, therefore, the court must make a preliminary reference (under Art 234 of the Treaty) to the ECJ, unless there is a judicial remedy available within UK law (in which case the court may still make a reference if it wishes). Once the answer is received, the English court must then apply it to the case. This is a very long and costly process, and the Member States have been keen to reduce the need to make references. A doctrine of 'acte clair' has developed in the ECJ case law, so that the court of the Member States can in certain circumstances (for example, where exactly the same question has been referred before) apply EC law without a reference being made. Lord

Denning was particularly keen to increase the efficiency of the process, and laid down some important principles in *HP Bulmer Ltd v J Bollinger SA* (1974):

- if a decision can be reached without a ruling, then there is no need to apply;

- if a similar case has been decided by the European Court, then there is need only to follow the precedent;

- if the point is clear, there is no need for a ruling, just apply the Treaty;

- the facts must be decided first before applying for a ruling;

- all the circumstances need to be taken into consideration – if applying for a ruling will cause delay, for example, or whether the parties wish to apply for a ruling.

Human Rights Act 1998

Under the 1998 Act, judges must construe all legislation, so far as possible, in a way which is compatible with the Convention. If it is impossible to do so, a declaration of incompatibility must be made.

4 The criminal courts and court procedure

Criminal appeals structure

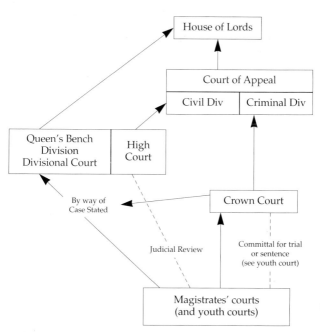

Magistrates' courts

With very few exceptions (for example, serious fraud cases), all criminal cases start in the magistrates' court. 98% of cases are dealt with solely by the magistrates' court. Magistrates (also called 'justices of the peace') try the following:

- summary offences, tried without a jury; petty motoring offences, theft, common assault, etc;

- indictable offences which are triable summarily at the option of the accused;

- magistrates conduct preliminary investigations of indictable offences to decide if there is a case to answer. If there is, the defendant is committed for trial to the Crown Court.

Committal proceedings

The Royal Commission on Criminal Justice argued that committal proceedings were not as effective as they should be. Old style committals have been abolished by s 44 of the Criminal Justice and Public Order Act 1994 and are now replaced by a new procedure of transfer of trial proceedings.

Now, s 51 of the Crime and Disorder Act 1998 states that, where an adult is charged with an offence triable only on indictment, the court shall send him directly to the Crown Court for trial. Where he is also charged with an either-way offence or a summary offence, he may be sent directly to trial for that as well, provided the magistrates believe that it is related to the indictable offence and, in the case of a summary offence, it is punishable with imprisonment or involves obligatory or discretionary disqualification from driving. The main practical effect of these changes is that defendants may now only use written evidence at the committal stage.

Composition of the court

Between two and seven justices of the peace may sit on the bench. Commonly the court is composed of either three justices of the peace, or one district judge (magistrates' court).

Jurisdiction

Magistrates have the power to imprison a convicted person for six months and can impose fines up to £5,000, as well as various community service orders. Magistrates can, if they think the offence is sufficiently serious to warrant a longer custodial sentence, commit the defendant to the Crown Court for sentencing.

The sentencing powers of all courts are now governed by the Powers of the Criminal Courts (Sentencing) Act 2000.

Police and Magistrates' Courts Act 1994

This Act has increased governmental interference in the police and magistrates' courts service in order to promote more efficiency in the administration of the police and courts. The Act gives new powers to the Home Secretary regarding the appointment of members of police authorities and accountability from chief constables.

Access to Justice Act 1999

Important changes to the magistrates' court system were made by the Access to Justice Act 1999.

The Act contains a range of provisions relating to magistrates and magistrates' courts:

    it provides for various changes to the organisation and management of magistrates' courts;

    it unifies the provincial and metropolitan stipendiary magistrates into a single bench;

    it removes the requirement for magistrates to sit on cases committed to the Crown Court for sentence and enables the Crown Court, rather than a magistrates' court, to deal with breaches of community sentences imposed by the Crown Court;

- it extends and clarifies the powers of civilians to execute warrants; this is intended to enable this function to be transferred from the police to the magistrates' courts.

The government's objective is to develop a magistrates' court service which is effectively and efficiently managed, at a local level by local people, within a consistent national framework. As part of this programme of reform, the Act includes provisions to:

- reform the organisation and management of the magistrates' courts by:

  o creating more flexible powers to alter the various territorial units that make up the magistrates' court service and to allow summary cases to be heard outside the commission area in which they arose;

  o expanding the potential membership of magistrates' courts committees by removing the limit on co-opted members;

  o establishing a single authority to manage the magistrates' courts service in London;

  o removing the requirement for justices' chief executives to be qualified lawyers and transferring responsibility for certain administrative functions from justices' clerks to justices' chief executives;

  o giving the Lord Chancellor power to require a MCCs to procure common goods and service where he considers this will lead to more effective efficient administration;

○ unify the provincial and metropolitan stipendiary benches into a single bench of district judges (magistrates' courts), able to sit in any magistrates' court in the country;

- remove the requirement for lay magistrates to sit as judges in the Crown Court on committals for sentence;

- extend and clarify the powers of civilians to execute warrants.

The new powers to change organisational units reflect the government's intention to develop a more coherent geographical structure for the criminal justice system as a whole. Common boundaries should enable the various criminal justice agencies to co-operate more effectively.

Crown Court

Crown Courts try:

- indictable only offences;

- either-way offences, where the accused has elected trial by jury.

The court is composed of a judge and a jury. See Chapter 7 for discussion of the jury system.

The Courts Act 1971 introduced the Crown Court. The Crown Court is part of the Supreme Court of Judicature (consisting of the Court of Appeal, the High Court of Justice and the Crown Court). There are three tiers:

- Queen's Bench Division (QBD) judges trying Class 1 offences (murder, treason, etc);

- second tier courts may have QBD judges or circuit judges and try Class 2 offences (rape, manslaughter, etc);

- third tier courts try Class 3 offences, with circuit judges or recorders in charge. Recorders are part time judges appointed on a temporary basis.

Classification of offences

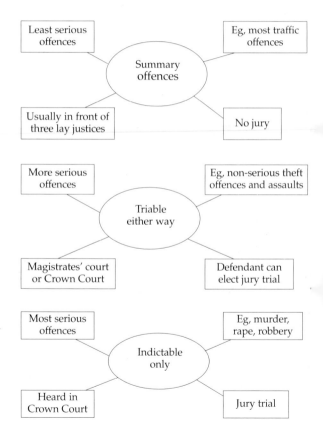

Least serious offences — Summary offences — Eg, most traffic offences

Usually in front of three lay justices — Summary offences — No jury

More serious offences — Triable either way — Eg, non-serious theft offences and assaults

Magistrates' court or Crown Court — Triable either way — Defendant can elect jury trial

Most serious offences — Indictable only — Eg, murder, rape, robbery

Heard in Crown Court — Indictable only — Jury trial

Statistics

The Crown Prosecution Service was set up in 1985 as the State's official prosecuting agency. In 1999, it underwent fundamental re-organisation and is now based on 42 regional units which correspond to those of the police services of England and Wales.

In its 2000–01 Annual Report (London: HMSO), the CPS states that, in the year under review, it dealt with 1.35 million cases in the magistrates' courts and around 116,000 in the Crown Court. The organisation is clearly under a certain pressure, as only 50.6% of committal papers were delivered to the defence within agreed timescales. The report notes that, in the magistrates' courts, the overall conviction rate was 98.3% (unchanged from the previous year). The conviction rate in the Crown Court was 87.9% compared with 88.6% in 1999–2000. These figures, though, represent cases which end up in court and they include guilty pleas. The number of discontinuances in both sorts of court is high. Discontinuances occur where witnesses fail to attend or attend and change their evidence. In 2000–01, there were 167,988 cases discontinued by the CPS in the magistrates' courts (13% of all cases brought – as compared to 12.2% the year before) and 10,145 cases not proceeded with in the Crown Court (12.3% of all cases brought, 529 more abandoned cases than the year before).

The document *Judicial Statistics 2000* (2001, Lord Chancellor's Department) notes that, during 2000, just under 67% of the defendants who pleaded not guilty to all counts were acquitted, representing almost 20% of the total 39,252 dealt with. Of these, just over 54% were discharged by the judge, 14% were acquitted on the direction of the judge and 32% were acquitted by a jury. Of the 9,672 defendants convicted in 2000 after a plea of not guilty to some or all counts, 21% were convicted on a majority verdict by a jury, the remainder being convicted unanimously.

High Court

This is structured in three divisions:

- Queen's Bench Division;
- Chancery Division; and
- Family Division.

The Access to Justice Act 1999 – jurisdiction

The Access to Justice Act 1999 establishes the jurisdiction of the High Court to hear cases stated by the Crown Court for an opinion of the High Court. It enables these and certain other applications to the High Court to be listed before a single judge. It provides for the appointment of a Vice President of the Queen's Bench Division. It also prohibits the publication of material likely to identify a child involved in proceedings under the Children Act 1989 before the High Court or a county court; and allows for under 14s to attend criminal trials.

Jurisdiction of single judge of High Court

The Act allows certain applications to be routinely heard by a single judge of the High Court. It does this by removing an obstacle that exists in the current legislation by which the route of appeal for these cases is to the House of Lords, but the Administration of Justice Act 1960 provides that the House of Lords will only hear appeals in these matters from a Divisional Court (that is, more than one judge) of the High Court. The 1999 Act amends the 1960 Act, so that the House of Lords can hear appeals from a single High Court judge. It will then be possible to make rules of court to provide for these cases to be heard by a single judge, while enabling the judge to refer particularly complex cases to a Divisional Court.

The cases in question include:

- appeals by way of case stated in criminal causes and matters;

- appeals from inferior (civil and criminal) courts and tribunals in contempt of court cases;

- criminal applications for habeas corpus.

Another change made by the 1999 Act concerns appeals from the Crown Court for opinion of High Court. The Supreme Court Act 1981 gives the High Court specific powers of disposal over appeals by way of case stated coming from a magistrates' court. However, it does not do the same for cases coming from the Crown Court. The Access to Justice Act 1999 provides a statutory footing for the powers of the High Court to deal with appeals by way of case stated coming from the Crown Court.

Judicial review

Where a party in magistrates' court proceedings wishes to complain of illegality, irrationality or procedural impropriety, an application for judicial review can be made. This course of action may be appropriate where it is the decision-making process that is at fault, rather than the actual decision. For consideration of the relationship between judicial review and appeals to the Crown Court, see *R v Hereford Magistrates' Court ex p Rowlands* (1997).

The Administrative Court has a discretionary power to grant three types of order – mandatory orders, quashing orders and prohibiting orders (formerly *mandamus*, *certiorari* and *prohibition*). The most common remedy sought in appeals from the magistrates' courts is a quashing order. This will be granted in three situations:

- where there is an error 'on the face of the record';
- where the court has acted in excess of jurisdiction;
- where the court has acted in breach of the rules of natural justice.

If granted, the decision of the magistrates will be quashed, and the court will usually direct that the case should be sent back to be heard by a differently constituted bench.

Court of Appeal

Appeals regarding criminal cases are sent to the Criminal Division of the Court of Appeal. The court hears appeals by the accused on questions of fact, questions of law, the sentence passed on the defendant and appeals by the prosecution on points of law (where an accused has been acquitted). The Criminal Appeal Act 1995 now states that an appeal from the Crown Court against conviction must have leave from the Court of Appeal.

Composition of court

The Lord Chief Justice, Lords Justices of Appeal and *puisne* judges (High Court judges) from the QBD.

House of Lords as a Court of Appeal

The Judicial Committee of the House of Lords is the highest Court of Appeal.

Composition of court

The Lord Chancellor, the Lords of Appeal in Ordinary, any other Law Lord who has held high judicial office.

Types of cases

Criminal matters from the Court of Appeal or a Divisional Court of the QBD, if leave to appeal has been granted from the lower court, or from the House itself.

The youth court

The youth court deals with offenders aged between 10 and 17 (Criminal Justice Act 1991), who must be considered in the context of the Children Act 1989. The Children Act 1989 gave statutory recognition to the need to avoid prosecution. Local authorities are required to take reasonable steps to reduce the need to bring criminal proceedings against children and young persons. The Criminal Justice Act 1991 identifies a number of changes, all in line with the welfare principle embodied in the Children Act:

s 70 renames the juvenile court the 'youth court';

 s 68 extends the jurisdiction so that the youth court and not the magistrates' court will deal with people under 18;

Pt III gives youth court magistrates new sentencing powers, together with a new scheme of past custody supervision;

English Legal System

- Pt I of the Act applies to offenders of all ages;

- the criteria for passing a custodial sentence are similar to those governing the use of custody for offenders under 21 which were contained in s 1(2) of the Criminal Justice Act 1982. These criteria helped reduce custodial sentences on juvenile offenders between 1980 and 1989.

Children under the age of 10 are irrebuttably presumed innocent. However, the courts now have limited power to grant orders which affect under-10s. The new orders are the *local child curfew* and the *child safety order*.

Section 34 of the Crime and Disorder Act 1998 brought 10–14 year olds within the criminal law by abolishing the rebuttable presumption of *doli incapax* for that age range. Now, prosecutions against 10–14 year olds will no longer have to prove that a defendant knew the difference between right and wrong before proceeding to prove the charge in issue.

The Act also abolished the system of cautioning in respect of young offenders who could be arrested but are not. A new 'final warning scheme' came into effect on 1 June 2000. As part of the new system, the Youth Justice and Criminal Evidence Act 1999 introduced a new sentencing power for magistrates in the youth court dealing with first-time offenders. They can now make a *referral order*, sending the juvenile to a *youth offender panel*.

The range of sentences available to the youth courts differs significantly from those available in the adult magistrates' court. There has been a trend in recent years of toughening sentences for children and young people. Since April 1999, the courts have been able to make detention and training orders (DTOs). A DTO may be used for 15–17 year olds who are convicted of a serious imprisonable offence. They may also be used for 12–14 year olds if they have record of persistent offending. The maximum term of any DTO is 24 months. Less severe penalties available to the youth courts are probation orders and supervision orders, which may be given to 16 or 17 year olds. The maximum amount of work which can be imposed in a community service order is 240 hours for offenders aged 16 and 17. Juveniles aged 16 can be compelled to attend an attendance centre for up to 36 hours.

Reform of the criminal courts

In 1999, Lord Justice Auld was commissioned by Lord Irvine LC to review how the criminal courts in England and Wales work at all levels. His final report was published in September 2001, and includes important wide-reaching recommendations for change. The government has allowed a 'period of comment' until the end of January 2002, following which a White Paper will be published. Below is a summary of the main recommendations. The full report can be found at www.criminal-courts-review.org.uk.

The criminal justice system

- A national Criminal Justice Board should replace all the existing national planning and operational bodies. Local Criminal Justice Boards should be responsible for giving effect to the national Board's directions and objectives and for management of the criminal justice system in their areas.

- A Criminal Justice Council, chaired by the Lord Chief Justice or senior Lord Justice of Appeal, should replace existing advisory and consultative bodies. It should have statutory power and duty to keep the criminal justice system under review.

A unified criminal court
- The Crown Court and magistrates' courts should be replaced by a unified criminal court consisting of three Divisions:

  ○ the Crown Division, constituted as the Crown Court now is (with a jury), to try all indictable-only matters and more serious 'either-way' offences;

  ○ the District Division, constituted by a judge (district judge or Recorder) and at least two lay magistrates (without a jury), exercising jurisdiction over mid-range 'either-way' offences of sufficient seriousness to merit up to two years' custody;

  ○ the Magistrates' Division, constituted as the magistrates' courts now are.

- The courts of the Magistrates' Division would decide on the venue for trial in each case. The defendant would have no right of election to be tried in any division. In the event of the present court structure continuing, the defendant should lose his right to elect mode of trial in either-way cases.

Juries
- See chapter on the jury system (Chapter 7).

The judiciary
- Except for Circuit Presiding Judges, the present rigid circuiteering pattern of High Court judges should be replaced by one in which they travel out to hear only the most important cases.

- There should be a strengthening in the training provided to judges.

Preparing for trial

- There should be improvements to the scheme of mutual disclosure established by the Criminal Procedure and Investigations Act 1996.

- There should be a move away from pre-trial hearings to co-operation between the parties according to standard timetables, wherever necessary seeking directions from the court.

The trial

- In trials by judge and jury, the judge, by reference to the case and issues summary, copies of which should be provided to the jury, should give them a fuller introduction to the case than is now conventional. Where he considers it appropriate he should require the jury publicly to answer each of a series of questions posed to them by him, and to declare a verdict in accordance with those questions.

- In trials by judge and magistrates, the judge should be the sole judge of the law, but he and the magistrates should together be the judges of fact, each having an equal vote.

- The law should, in general, move way from technical rules of inadmissibility to trusting judicial and lay fact finders to give relevant evidence the weight it deserves.

- The criminal courts should be equipped with an online sentencing information system.

Appeals

There should be a single line of appeal from the Magistrates' Division and above to the Court of Appeal.

- The Law Commission's recommendations for the introduction of statutory exceptions to the double jeopardy rule should be implemented, subject to some minor alterations. There should be provision for appeal by the defence or the prosecution against a verdict of the jury which is perverse.

- Measures should be introduced to increase the efficiency of the Court of Appeal in dealing with matters of general public importance or of particular complexity, and 'straightforward' appeals.

The investigation of crime

The 'criminal justice system' has been the subject of heated parliamentary and academic debate in recent years. The uncovering of many miscarriages of justice in the 1980s and 1990s, and the ever-increasing prison population in the face of rising crime figures has led many people to mistrust the police and the system as a whole. A Royal Commission on Criminal Justice was set up in 1991, one of the most significant results of which was the setting up of the Criminal Cases Review Commission to investigate suspected miscarriages of justice. During the 1990s, however, confidence in the police continued to fall, and it plummeted sharply following the publication of the Macpherson Report in February 1999.

The Macpherson Report

Sir William Macpherson was commissioned to lead a judicial inquiry into the police's failure to investigate properly the racist killing of the black London teenager Stephen Lawrence. The report is most often quoted for its finding that the Metropolitan Police was infected by 'institutional racism', but it identified numerous fundamental failings of the police. Its main recommendations were:

- that the principle against 'double jeopardy' should be abolished. The report recommended that the Court of Appeal should have the power to permit prosecution after acquittal for the same offence 'where fresh and viable evidence is presented'. The trial of the five suspects in the Lawrence case was stopped because there was insufficient evidence to proceed. The defendants were acquitted, and there is a widespread feeling that the guilty have got away with a serious and repulsive crime;

- that a ministerial priority should be established for all police services 'to increase trust and confidence in policing among minority ethnic communities';

- that a Freedom of Information Act should apply to all areas of policing, subject only to a 'substantial harm' test for withholding information;

- that the Race Relations Acts should apply to all police officers;

- that the CPS and the police should take particular care to recognise any evidence of racial motivation in a crime.

Largely as a result of this report, Parliament passed the Race Relations (Amendment) Act 2000, which gives all public authorities a duty to:

(a) seek to eliminate unlawful discrimination; and

(b) promote equality of opportunity.

The rest of this chapter looks at police powers, pre-trial procedures, and the rights of those charged with criminal offences.

Arrest

The normal method of arrest is under a warrant issued by a magistrate or higher judicial officer (s 1 of the Magistrates' Courts Act 1980).

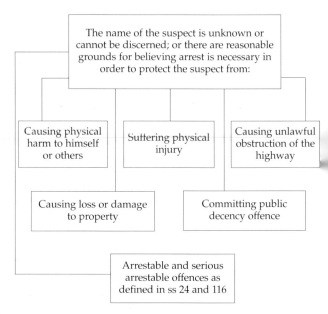

The name of the suspect is unknown or cannot be discerned; or there are reasonable grounds for believing arrest is necessary in order to protect the suspect from:

Causing physical harm to himself or others

Suffering physical injury

Causing unlawful obstruction of the highway

Causing loss or damage to property

Committing public decency offence

Arrestable and serious arrestable offences as defined in ss 24 and 116

Arrest without a warrant

A constable can arrest without warrant if there is reasonable ground for believing that an arrestable offence has been committed or when general arrest provisions exist. Under s 24 of the Police and Criminal Evidence Act (PACE) 1984, the police have wide powers to arrest without warrant.

Arrest for non-arrestable offences

Only the police have this power. This can be done if any of the general arrest conditions under s 25(3) of PACE are satisfied.

Powers of arrest (s 24)

Section 24 of PACE defines the powers of arrest:

- anyone may summarily arrest (without warrant) any person who is reasonably suspected of committing an arrestable offence or is actually committing such an offences, or any person who has committed an arrestable offence or is reasonably suspected to have done so;

- the police may also arrest a person who is about to commit an arrestable offence (*Hussein v Chong Fook Kam* (1970)). 'Suspicion' was defined as a state of conjecture where proof is lacking (*James v Chief Constable of South Wales Police Force* (1991)). Under s 116, an arrestable offence could become a serious arrestable offence if there is:

  ○ serious harm to State security or public order;

  ○ serious interference with the administration of justice in a particular case;

  ○ serious injury or death, or substantial gain or loss.

An arrest will be unlawful where the reasons given by the arresting officer point to an offence for which no power of arrest is given (or for which there is only qualified power of arrest) and it is clear that no other reasons were present to the mind of the officer (*Edwards v DPP* (1993)). This principle was confirmed in *Mullady v DPP* (1997). A police officer arrested M for 'obstruction', an offence with the power of arrest only if the defendant's conduct amounted to a breach of the peace (for which there is a common law power of arrest) or if one of the general arrest conditions, as set out in s 25, is satisfied. The police argued that the officer could have arrested M for a breach of the peace and merely gave the wrong reason. The Divisional Court held that the officer had acted unlawfully and that it would be wrong for the justices to go behind the reason given and infer that the reason for the arrest was another lawful reason.

Common law arrest for breach of the peace

Under common law, any individual can arrest anyone who is committing a breach of the peace. A constable can arrest anyone who is obstructing him in the execution of his duty and can call upon the general public to assist him, using reasonable force if necessary; there is no need for arrest to be followed by a charge. The person can be released without being able to claim that he has been falsely imprisoned (*Holgate-Mohammed v Duke* (1984)).

The power of the police to enter and deal with a breach of the peace is embodied in a number of cases (*McConnell v Chief Constable of the Greater Manchester Police* (1990); *Howell* (1981); *Lamb v DPP* (1989)).

Arrest procedures

When an arrest is made, the arresting officer must make it clear to the individual that he is being arrested and state the reasons for the arrest. If this is not possible, then the person being arrested should be informed as soon as practicable to do so (s 28 of PACE). If these rules are not observed, it could render the arrest unlawful:

- s 29 of PACE deals with arrests made while the individual is at the police station voluntarily;

- s 30 embodies the general requirement whereby an individual must be taken as soon as possible to a police station after arrest.

Duties of the custody officer

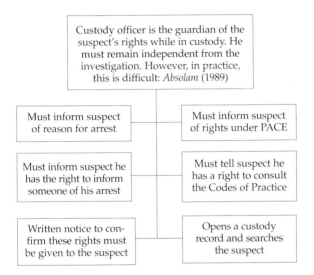

Custody officer is the guardian of the suspect's rights while in custody. He must remain independent from the investigation. However, in practice, this is difficult: *Absolam* (1989)

Must inform suspect of reason for arrest

Must inform suspect of rights under PACE

Must inform suspect he has the right to inform someone of his arrest

Must tell suspect he has a right to consult the Codes of Practice

Written notice to confirm these rights must be given to the suspect

Opens a custody record and searches the suspect

Helping with inquiries

The police do not have the power to detain an individual in order to assist them with their inquiries. The person must be actually arrested (*Lemsatef* (1977)).

Section 29 of PACE states that a person who attends a police station to assist the police in their inquiries has the right to leave at any time, if not arrested by the police. There is no legal duty on the police to point this fact out to the person. It is obviously in the interests of the police to gather as much information as they can before charging the suspect. The protection of a suspect's rights under PACE does not come into effect until the suspect has been arrested and, therefore, it is in the interests of the arresting officer to delay arrest.

Delay of arrest

Though the police are under no legal duty to inform the suspect of his rights prior to arrest, if it is thought that the delay in arresting the suspect was to deliberately circumvent the protections under PACE, a court may exclude any confession which results from the interview (*Ismail* (1990)).

Booking in

When a police officer detains a suspect, he must be taken as soon as is practicable to a designated police station. Section 36 of PACE provides that the designated station must have a custody officer normally of the rank of sergeant. It is the custody officer who will make the decision whether to detain the suspect.

Searching the suspect

The custody officer searches the suspect and details of the suspect's property are recorded in the custody record. Personal items are usually retained by the suspects (not money or valuables). The custody officer can retain any articles with which he believes the suspect may cause injury to himself or others.

Intimate body searches

A strip search can be carried out if this is necessary. Intimate body searches can be carried out with the permission of an officer at least of the rank of superintendent. Intimate searches for drugs or harmful objects should be undertaken by a nurse or doctor or, if not practicable, by an officer of the same sex. Section 117 allows the police to use reasonable force to search.

Detention without charge

As seen, it is in the interests of the police to detain a suspect without charge for as long as possible in order to gain further information about the offence committed. The rules governing interviewing of suspects are contained in the Codes of Practice. Meals, refreshment and rest breaks must be given to the suspect during his detention.

Vulnerable suspects

The Codes of Practice state that the police cannot obtain answers to questions by using tricks or oppression and vulnerable suspects must be accorded certain rights. The custody officer must arrange for an 'appropriate adult' to attend if the suspect being interviewed is:

- a juvenile;

- blind;

- mentally handicapped; or

- unable to read.

The suspect can object to the appropriate adult being present (*DPP v Blake* (1989)). If the suspect is mentally handicapped and makes a confession with no 'appropriate adult' present, the confession may be excluded. If the judge admits the confession, he must give a warning to the jury on the danger of convicting on the basis of the confession (*Lamont* (1989)).

Medical treatment

The custody officer must arrange for medical treatment if a suspect requires it. If a doctor deems a suspect unfit to be interviewed, then a further medical examination should be given before the suspect is interviewed. However, failure to obtain a subsequent medical examination will not breach the Code in itself (*Trussler* (1988)).

Failure to observe these principles may result in any confession being rendered inadmissible in evidence (*Everett* (1988); *DPP v Blake* (1989)).

Time limits

There are strict time limits on the detention of suspects without charge. An arrested person may not be detained without charge for more than 24 hours unless a serious arrestable offence has been committed. It can be extended to 36 hours by a superintendent, to secure or preserve evidence. If a serious arrestable offence has been committed and the suspect has been detained for 36 hours, the police must bring him before a magistrates' court to extend the time limit to a maximum of 60 hours.

Review periods

There must be regular review periods of the detention of the suspect. If the suspect has not been charged, the review officer must be at least the rank of inspector and the first review should be carried out no later than six hours from detention; then, every nine hours. If the suspect is charged, the custody officer has the responsibility of review.

Delay in exercising suspect's rights

If a suspect is detained in the police station, he has the right to have a friend or relative informed of his arrest. An officer of the rank of superintendent (or acting rank) (*Alladice* (1988)) can delay the exercise of these rights under s 56(1) of PACE if:

Delay must be communicated to the suspect and recorded in the custody record. When the delay ends, the suspect must be informed of this fact: *Walsh* (1989); *Cochrane* (1988)

Suspect is detained for a serious arrestable offence

Officer of at least the rank of superintendent authorises it

Could obstruct the recovery of property obtained as a result of such an offence

When suspect exercises his rights, it may lead to interference with or harm to evidence connected with a serious arrestable offence

Grounds for delay

- It is not sufficient ground for delay that an accomplice of the suspect was still at large and might be alerted because the arrest was made in a public place in front of people known to the suspect (*Alladice* (1988)).

- It was not sufficient ground for delay when the suspect's mother had been informed of the arrest by telephone before the decision to delay access to a solicitor had been made (*Samuel* (1988)).

- The police cannot delay access to a solicitor on the ground that access may prejudice police inquiries. Access to a solicitor (s 58 of PACE) is a fundamental safeguard under the Act.

Legal advice at the police station

In *Samuel* (1988), Hodgson LJ commented that the right of access to a solicitor for suspects in police custody is 'one of the most important and fundamental rights of a citizen'.

Section 58(1) of PACE provides that:

> A person arrested and held in custody ... shall be entitled, if he so requests, to consult a solicitor privately at any time.

A suspect is entitled to consult the duty solicitor if he so wishes. However, the role of the lawyer in the police station has been the subject of much debate. Recent research for the Royal Commission on Criminal Justice by Professor John Baldwin, *The Role of Legal Representatives at Police Stations* (1993), concludes that, on the whole, solicitors are performing badly at police interviews. They tend to adopt a passive role, rather than confronting issues on behalf of their client.

Duty solicitor scheme

The duty solicitor arrangements came into force in April 1990. Important changes centred on the duties of the solicitor in responding to a call:

- previously, a duty solicitor on a rota basis had to accept a call from the regional telephone service. Whether he would attend personally at the police station was at his discretion;

- the new arrangements state that a duty solicitor on a rota, or a panel duty solicitor who accepts a call, must provide initial advice to suspects who have asked for the duty solicitor, by talking to them directly on the telephone. The only circumstances where initial telephone advice does not have to be given are:

○ where the solicitor is already at or near to the police station and can provide advice to the suspect immediately;

○ the suspect is not capable of speaking to the solicitor because of intoxication or violent behaviour; in these cases, the solicitor must arrange to provide the initial advice as soon as is practicable.

When the initial advice is provided, the solicitor must attend the suspect at the police station:

If suspect requests this	If police intend to hold an identification parade
If suspect has been arrested for an offence under s 24 of PACE 1984 and the police wish to question him	If suspect complains of serious maltreatment by the police

Interviews: conduct and control

Absolam (1989) stated:

> There was not, in any formal sense, a conventional interview ... but, equally, it was an interview within the provisions of the Code, in that it was a series of

questions directed by the police to the suspect, with a view to obtaining admissions on which proceedings could be founded.

There has been much debate as to what actually constitutes 'an interview'. The Report of the Royal Commission on Criminal Justice (1993), para 38, recommends that:

> The definition of an interview in Code C Note for Guidance 11A should be clarified to remove the apparent confusion as to what constitutes an interview for the purposes of the Code.

In *Chung* (1991), the defendant was questioned at his flat. He was arrested and asked to consult his solicitor, but was denied. He was allowed access to his solicitor only after he confessed. His confession was excluded under s 76(2)(b). The evidence was also inadmissible under s 78 (*Absolam* (1989)).

In *Davis* (1990), the statutory procedure under ss 7 and 8 of the Road Traffic Act 1988 with respect to obtaining a breathalyser test from a driver did not constitute an interview for the purposes of Code C. Evidence was wrongly excluded by justices under s 78 of PACE (see, further, *Langiert* (1991); *DPP v McGladrigan* (1991)).

Confession evidence and admissibility

The general principles developed by the courts to govern interviews are:

- suspects must be cautioned before an interview takes place;

- on every new occasion a suspect is exposed to police questioning, he should be given a further caution (*Brown (Kingsley)* (1989));

- the provisions of PACE must be complied with, particularly in respect of meal breaks and rest periods;

- interviews at police stations must be recorded contemporaneously, unless impracticable to do so;

- a record should be made as soon as possible and it must be shown why it was impracticable for the police officer to have made the record at the appropriate time (*Delaney* (1988));

- the record of the interview must be shown to the suspect if the suspect is still in custody at the completion of the record;

- methods employed by the police to obtain evidence must not be used in circumstances which may result in the confession being obtained oppressively, by threats or by bribes.

If there are any doubts about the reliability of police evidence regarding a confession, this can lead to the exclusion of the confession evidence under ss 78 and 76(2)(b).

- *Delaney* (1988):

  failure by the police to make a contemporary record or failure to show it to the suspect can cast doubt on police evidence, since the confession may have been tampered with in some way;

- *Khan (Hassan)* (1990):

  failure by the police to record interviews causes difficulties for the court when allegations of 'verballing' a suspect are made against the police (*Keenan* (1990));

- *Canale* (1990):

  a confession can be inadmissible if it is obtained by 'oppression' under s 76(2)(A) (*Emmerson* (1991); *Doolan* (1988); *Howard Chung* (1992); *Crampton* (1991); *Goldenberg* (1988)).

Entrapment

There exists no clear authority to determine whether s 78 of PACE allows the exclusion of evidence if an offence is instigated by the police acting as *agents provocateurs* (*Sang* (1979)), even though the courts have disapproved of these methods (*Brannan v Peek* (1948)).

However, s 78 could have prompted some change in *Gill and Ranuana* (1989). Lord Lane stated:

  ... nevertheless, we have no doubt that the speeches in *Sang* and the import of those speeches are matters to be taken into account by a judge when applying the provisions of s 78.

Identification parades

The general principle is that, if the suspect wishes for an identification parade to take place, it must be done unless it would be impracticable to do so. The police must ensure that the parade is fair and any identification of a suspect which is made must be reliable. Breaches of these procedures can lead to the evidence being excluded under s 78 of PACE.

Royal Commission's recommendations

The Commission recommended that:

- if the prosecution evidence is deemed unsafe or unsatisfactory, the judge should be able to stop the case;

- if a confession has been made by the suspect away from the police station, the suspect should be presented with it at the beginning of the first tape recorded interview made at the police station;

- where confession evidence is involved in a case, a judicial warning should be issued.

Criminal Evidence (Northern Ireland) Order 1988

The right to silence in Northern Ireland has been abolished since 1988. It is possible for a court to draw inferences from a defendant's silence at the police station and from him failing to account for his presence at a particular place; or from marks or items found on the defendant which may link him to a crime.

It is further proposed that judges should comment to the jury on a refusal to take the oath or answer questions.

Bail

The question of bail can arise at the police station and again when the accused appears before the court. Bail is defined as:

> The release of a person subject to a duty to surrender to custody at a particular time and place.

Arrest under warrant

If a person has been arrested by warrant, the warrant will usually have provisions included as to whether bail should be granted. The decision is made by the magistrate who issues the warrant.

Arrest not under warrant

If arrest is not under warrant, the police must act in accordance with the provisions contained in PACE.

Under PACE, the custody officer is responsible for deciding whether to continue the detention of a suspect who has not been charged. After being charged, a person must be released unless:

- the police cannot discover the person's name and address or believe that the information given is false;

- the police reasonably believe that detention is necessary for the person's protection or to prevent the person causing harm to someone else or interfering with property; or

- the police reasonably believe that the person will 'jump bail', interfere with witnesses or otherwise obstruct the course of justice.

Bail from court

The granting of bail from court is governed by the Bail Act 1976. Section 4 governs the accused's right to bail. Section 4 gives a right to bail in those cases which do not come within Sched 1 of the Bail Act.

The exceptions to bail are classed in two lists:

- the first list will apply if the defendant is charged with an offence which carries a possible custodial sentence;

- the second list applies if the offence is one which does not carry a custodial sentence.

If it is an imprisonable offence, the court does not have to grant bail if it believes that the defendant may:

Fail to surrender to custody	Commit an offence while out on bail	Interfere with witnesses or otherwise obstruct the course of justice

The Criminal Justice and Public Order Act (CJPOA) 1994 restricts the granting of bail if the defendant commits another offence while already out on bail.

Appeal against refusal to grant bail

An accused person can appeal to the High Court against a magistrates' decision not to grant bail. An accused person not granted bail can also appeal to the Crown Court, which can grant bail if:

- the magistrates have remanded the defendant in custody after a full bail application has been made;

- if the magistrates have committed the defendant to the Crown Court for trial or sentence; or

- if the magistrates have convicted the accused and refused him bail pending appeal to the Crown Court.

Stop and search

The police powers regarding search of an individual are contained in the Police and Criminal Evidence Act 1984 and the Home Office Codes of Practice.

Under s 1 of PACE, a police officer can stop, detain and search any person that he reasonably suspects may be carrying stolen or prohibited items and seize them. Articles would include offensive weapons; and articles made and adapted for use in connection with an offence, such as burglary, theft, taking of a motor vehicle or obtaining property by deception.

PACE concentrates the main powers of the police in respect of stop and search, but there are other statutes which exist before and after PACE which allow the police this power:

- Misuse of Drugs Act 1971;

- Firearms Act 1968;

- Aviation Security Act 1982;

- Crossbows Act 1987;

- Prevention of Terrorism (Temporary Provisions) Act 1989.

Section 2 of PACE provides safeguards for the suspect and indicates the extent to which a police officer can search a suspect in a public place. Section 117 allows a police officer to use reasonable force in the exercise of his powers.

Under s 163 of the Road Traffic Act 1988, a police officer has the power to stop any motor vehicle.

Powers under s 60 of the CJPOA 1994

Section 60 of the CJPOA 1994 created new stop and search powers in anticipation of violence. The powers must be authorised by a senior officer and must be limited to where there is a fear of an outbreak of violence. The authorising officer must reasonably believe that it is 'expedient' to give an authorisation in order to prevent the occurrence of incidents of serious violence. Thus, the authorisation need not be the only way in which such serious incidents may be prevented. Various policing factors may have to be balanced, including the ability of the police force to remain effective and efficient if it were to use other methods.

The scope of s 60 of the CJPOA 1994 and police powers to stop and search are being incrementally extended through various Acts of Parliament. They include the following: s 8 of the Knives Act 1997 amended s 60 to allow *initial* authorisations by an inspector or above, thus obviating the need for an officer of at least the rank of superintendent; s 60(1)(b) extended the criteria under which an authorising officer may invoke this power to include reasonable belief that incidents involving serious violence may take place or that such instruments of weapons are being carried in a particular area; and s 60(3) provided that authorisations may be extended up to 24 hours, instead of six, although only an officer of the rank of superintendent or above may do this. A new sub-section, sub-s 11A, was inserted under s 60 by s 8 of the 1997 Knives Act and stated that: '... for the purposes of this section, a person carries a dangerous instrument or an offensive weapon if he has it in his possession.' These amendments are intended to deal with anticipated violence in situations where gangs or persons may be 'tooled-up' and travelling through various police areas *en route* to an intended scene of confrontation. Thus, the power may be invoked, even where it is believed that the actual anticipated violence may occur in another police jurisdiction, for example, by football hooligans travelling to and from matches.

Further amendments to s 60 were made under the Crime and Disorder Act (CDA) 1998. This is mainly to deal with the problem of troublemakers deliberately wearing facial coverings to conceal their identities, especially when the police are using CCTV cameras.

Section 81 of the CJPOA 1994

Section 81 creates a new power of stop and search of persons and vehicles where it is expedient to do so to prevent certain acts of terrorism. Any officer of or above the rank of commander or assistant chief constable may authorise a stop and search where 'it appears to him to be expedient to do so' in order to prevent acts of terrorism connected with Northern Ireland, or international terrorism.

The Code of Practice (A) for the exercise of statutory powers of stop and search

In view of the wide powers vested in the police in the exercise of stop and search, Code A was revised to reflect the new legislation and to clarify how searches under stop and search powers are to be conducted. The revised Code came into effect in 1999 and supersedes the edition of Code A which came into effect in 1997.

Code (1AA) restates the guidance under the previous edition and emphasises:

> It is important to ensure that the powers of stop and search are used responsibly by those who exercise them and those who authorise their use. It is also particularly important to ensure that any person searched is treated courteously and considerately.

Code A states, in relation to the ability of an officer to search a person in the street with his consent, where no search power exists, that:

> In these circumstances, an officer should always make it clear that he is seeking the consent of the person concerned to the search being carried out, by telling the person that he need not consent and that without his consent he will not be searched.

Entry, search and seizure

Section 8 of PACE provides for a general power for magistrates to issue search warrants to the police where there are reasonable grounds for believing that a 'serious arrestable offence' has been committed. The police must have reasonable grounds to suspect that admissible evidence in connection with the offence will be found on the premises and that:

- it is not reasonably practicable to contact any person who could give permission to enter the premises;

- such a person has unreasonably refused to allow the police to enter the premises or hand over the evidence;

- evidence would be hidden, removed or destroyed if the police sought access without a warrant.

Certain articles, such as articles which are subject to legal privilege (that is, between a client and his solicitor), cannot be seized under a warrant. Excluded material includes personal records, such as medical records, specimens for medical purposes and certain journalistic material held in confidence.

In *Central Criminal Court ex p AJD Holdings* (1992), the court stressed that, when police officers request a warrant, they should be clear what evidence it is hoped a search will reveal; further, the application should make it clear how the material relates to the crime which is under investigation.

In *Billericay Justices and Dobbyn ex p Harris Coaches* (1991), a police officer had the power to require the production of documents in pursuance of s 99 of the Transport Act 1968. The officer had, instead, chosen to proceed under the powers in ss 8 and 15 of PACE. The Divisional Court refused the application for judicial review of the magistrates' decision to issue a search warrant.

A search under a warrant 'may only be a search to the extent required for the purpose of which the warrant was issued' (s 16(8)). In *Chief Constable of the Warwickshire Constabulary ex p Fitzpatrick* (1998), the Divisional Court disapproved of the police practice of using a warrant phrased in broad terms to seize every possible item that could broadly fall within those terms. They should ensure both that the material seized falls within the terms of the warrant and, because such a warrant is granted to search for material of evidential value, that there are reasonable grounds for believing so and to be likely to be of substantial value in the investigation. In this case, in relation to one of the warrants, the police officers went on a 'fishing expedition' and seized a large selection of documents not, on their face, related to the offence under investigation. In doing so, they exceeded the ambit of the warrant.

Entry and search without a warrant

Section 18 of PACE 1984 provides the police with the power to enter and search. These provisions relate to entry and search after the arrest for an arrestable offence of a person who occupies or controls the premises, so that further evidence connected with the offence may be obtained. Section 32 allows the police to enter and search any premises if a suspect is arrested away from the police station and was at the premises on or prior to the arrest, in order to search for evidence of the offence committed.

Where evidence of entry and search after arrest is admitted, it is a question for the jury, not the judge, whether the actual purpose of the police officer's search was to search for such evidence. In *Beckford* (1991), confirmation was given by the

Court of Appeal that, under s 32, the police can enter and search premises if the defendant had been in those premises shortly before arrest. The officer's credibility in respect of the search could be tested by the reasons given for the search.

Terrorism Act 2000

The Terrorism Act 2000 replaced the 'temporary' provisions contained in the Prevention of Terrorism Act 1989. It gives exceptional stop and search powers to the police. An officer of at least the rank of commander or assistant chief constable, who considers it expedient to do so for the prevention of terrorism, may issue an authorisation specifying a particular area or place. While the order is in effect (no more than 28 days), uniformed officers have the power to stop and search any vehicle or person within that area. 'Terrorism' is not very clearly defined, but includes a whole range of acts if they are designed to influence the government or to intimidate a section of the public, and made for the purpose of advancing a political, religious or ideological cause. The Act has caused much concern among civil liberties groups, who fear that it may be used to control all kinds of disaffected groups who would not normally be branded as 'terrorists' by the general public.

The Anti-terrorism, Crime and Security Act 2001 includes new powers of indefinite detention in relation to people suspected of involvement with 'terrorist groups'. In order for such wide powers of detention to be clearly lawful under the Human Rights Act 1998, the government had to invoke Art 15, which allows derogations from Art 5 (the right to liberty and security) 'in time of war or other public emergency threatening the life of the nation'. The government controversially considered that the UK was in such a time following the terrorist attacks on 11 September

2001. The proposed legislation also includes limitations on the right to judicial review in certain immigration matters. The derogation from the European Convention and the specific provisions of the Bill have been strongly criticised by many lawyers and civil liberties groups.

Adverse inference from silence

Following the enactment of the CJPOA 1994, there has been a steady stream of case law as to correct judicial practice when directing the jury about the drawing of adverse inferences under ss 34 and 35.

In *R v Cowan* (1995), the Court of Appeal considered what should be said in the summing up if the defendant decides not to testify. The jury must be directed that (as provided by s 38(3) of the CJPOA 1994) an inference from failure to give evidence could not, on its own, prove guilt. The jury had to be satisfied (on the basis of the evidence called by the prosecution) that the prosecution had established a case to answer before inferences could be drawn from the accused's silence. The jury could only draw an adverse inference from the accused's silence if it concluded that the silence could only be sensibly attributed to the accused having no answer to the charge or none that could stand up to cross-examination.

The difficult issue as to correct judicial practice when the accused remains silent during interview on the advice of his solicitor was considered in *R v Condron* (1997) and *R v Argent* (1997). These cases make it clear that such advice was only one factor to be taken into consideration, along with all the other circumstances, in any jury determination as to whether adverse inferences could be drawn from a 'no comment' interview. In *Condron,* the Court of Appeal considered the guidelines set out in *Cowan* (above) and concluded that they were equally applicable to failure to answer questions (s 34) and failure to testify (s 35). The Court of Appeal approved the Judicial Studies Board specimen direction which states:

> If he failed to mention when he was questioned [a fact which he relied on in his defence], decide whether, in the circumstances which existed at the time, it was a fact he could have reasonably be expected then to mention.

The law is that as a juror you may draw such inferences as appear proper from the defendant's failure to mention something at that time. You do not have to hold it against him. It is for a juror to decide whether it is proper to do so.

It is also desirable to direct the jury that if, despite any evidence relied upon to explain the failure (to answer questions) or in the absence of such evidence, they concluded that the failure could only sensibly be attributed to the accused having fabricated the evidence subsequently, they might draw an adverse inference.

The Youth Justice and Criminal Evidence Act 1999 amends s 34 by adding a new s 34(2A). This prohibits the drawing of adverse inferences from silence at a police station where the suspect was not allowed an opportunity to consult a solicitor prior to being questioned or charged.

Instituting proceedings

Prosecutions are usually brought by the Crown Prosecution Service, established by s 1 of the Prosecution of Offences Act 1985. The Crown Prosecution Service works independently from the police: *they* take the decision to prosecute, not police officers. Under s 6 of the Prosecution of Offences Act 1985, a private individual can institute a prosecution.

Laying an information

A prosecution can be started by laying an information – either written or oral – or by charging a person with an offence, which is contained in a charge sheet.

5　The civil process

Key differences in civil and criminal law

Public law
This includes criminal law, constitutional and administrative law. Public law is concerned with the interaction between an individual and the rest of the community.

Private law
This includes tort, contract and divorce law. Private law concerns the interaction between individuals in that community, inasmuch as they do not concern the community as a whole.

It is possible to be both liable in public and private law.

Criminal law is concerned with conduct of which the State disapproves and will punish the wrongdoer, seeking to deter others from similar behaviour.

Civil law has a complementary function. When a dispute arises between two individuals, rules of civil law are applied to determine which individual is in the right. The party in the wrong must then compensate the other for any loss or damage.

The object of the criminal law is, therefore, punitive; the object of the civil law is to compensate the person wronged.

Separate court systems

There are separate systems of courts dealing with criminal and civil cases.

Courts exercising civil jurisdiction

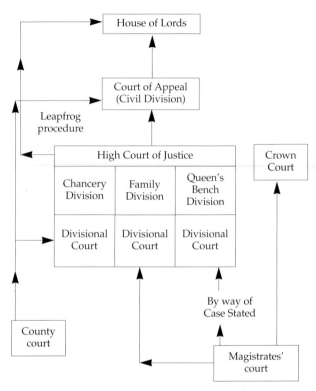

Note: Appeals are indicated thus ────────▶

The magistrates' court

Magistrates deal with a large volume of civil cases, in particular with family matters. They deal with issues such as:

- judicial separation;
- maintenance payments;
- affiliation orders;
- guardianship of minors;
- adoption orders;
- case orders.

They also have many administrative tasks, such as issuing and renewing licences, dealing with community charge enforcements and recovery of certain civil debts. The Children Act 1989 has widened the jurisdiction of the magistrates in respect of child law and jurisdiction under the youth court (previously the juvenile court) for juveniles under 17 years of age.

County courts

Established in 1846, county courts provide a cheap system of local justice staffed by circuit judges and district judges.

The High Court
The High Court consists of:

The High Court is split into three basic divisions, each of which is further divided. Any *puisne* judge can deal with any High Court matter, but they tend to specialise.

The Chancery Division
First instance jurisdiction consists of:

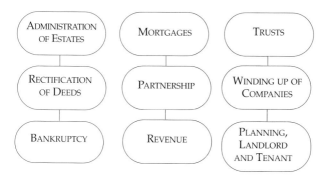

On occasions, other cases are dealt with by other courts, for example:

The courts' appellate jurisdiction hears appeals from decisions of the Inland Revenue Commissioners, and appeals on bankruptcy and land registration cases from the county courts.

The Family Division

Created by the Administration of Justice Act 1970. First instance jurisdiction covers:

- family matters (including all cases concerning marriage – its validity and termination; legitimacy; wardship; adoption; guardianship, custodianship; and family property disputes);

- all issues concerning proceedings under the Children Act 1989; proceedings under the Domestic Violence and Matrimonial Proceedings Act 1976; and s 30 of the Human Fertilisation and Embryology Act 1990.

The court's appellate jurisdiction hears appeals from:

- county courts;
- magistrates' courts; and
- Crown Courts.

The Queen's Bench Division

Largest of the three divisions. Presided over by the Lord Chief Justice. First instance jurisdiction consists of:

- contract actions;
- tort actions.

The division also includes the Admiralty Court dealing with claims for injury or loss through collisions at sea.

Also includes the Commercial Court, dealing with claims for insurance, banking, agency and negotiable instruments.

The appellate jurisdiction of the High Court is as follows:

- single judge can hear appeals from certain tribunals, and from commercial arbitrators, particularly on points of law;
- Divisional Court of two judges has a certain civil appeal function, for example, from the Solicitor's Disciplinary Tribunal;
- also hears appeals from magistrates' court, which have been to the Crown Court for appeal or sentence, by way of a 'case stated';

- it oversees the activities of all the inferior courts. Can issue three types of prerogative orders and one prerogative unit: mandamus; certiorari; prohibition; habeas corpus.

The House of Lords

- Supreme court of appeal for civil cases in Great Britain and Northern Ireland.

- Appeal to the House of Lords requires leave of the Court of Appeal or, in certain cases, from the High Court or Divisional Court, for leapfrog appeal under the provisions of the Administration of Justice Act.

- Appeals to the House are generally only permitted if there is a point of law of general public importance.

- Appeal committees consist of three Law Lords who report their recommendations to the Appellate Committee.

Judicial Committee of the Privy Council

The Committee hears appeals from Ecclesiastical Courts and certain professional tribunals. Members of the Committee consist of:

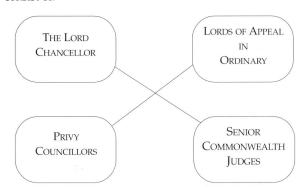

European Court of Justice

If there is an issue in a case concerning the interpretation of community law, the court must refer the case to the European Court for a ruling (Art 234 of the EC Treaty, formerly Art 177).

Organisation of civil courts

There have been many changes in the organisation of civil courts following the recommendations of the Civil Justice Review, initiated in 1985, to speed up the process and improve access to justice.

The Civil Justice Review was concerned to meet the public's criticisms that justice was too slow, inaccessible, very expensive, and extremely complex in its process.

Reform of civil litigation

In February 1985, the then Lord Chancellor, Lord Hailsham, began a review into the machinery of civil justice. The Review was undertaken by the Lord Chancellor's Department under the supervision of an advisory committee chaired by Sir Maurice Hodgson. The review centred on five consultative papers concerning civil litigation:

- personal injury;
- small claims;
- Commercial Court;
- debt enforcement;
- housing.

The final report was published in 1988. Its findings were implemented in the Courts and Legal Services Act 1990.

There has been criticism of the controversial redistribution of court business. The Civil Justice Review had concluded that too many personal injury cases were going through the High Court, cases which were in fact straightforward, and there was no need to take up valuable High Court time. Only 36% of awards at trial and 14% of settlements in the High Court were for sums exceeding £20,000. The biggest problem was the delay in the High Court, litigants waiting up to five years or more. The High Court was to be reserved for public law and specialised cases.

Stephen Sedley QC in 'Improving civil justice' (1990) *Civil Justice Quarterly* stated that:

> ... these measures were to allow for a 'judicial fast track' for public law, particularly commercial cases, at the expense of issues arising from things like accidents at work or on the road, wrongful arrests, contracts of employment or tenancies and housing conditions – in other words, individuals' problems.

The Woolf reforms 1999
When Lord Woolf began his examination of the civil law process, the problems facing those who used the system were many and varied. His Interim Report published in June 1995 identified these problems. He noted, for example, that:

> ... the key problems facing civil justice today are cost, delay and complexity. These three are interrelated and stem from the uncontrolled nature of the litigation process. In particular, there is no clear judicial responsibility for managing individual cases or for the overall administration of the civil courts. Just as the problems are

interrelated, so too the solutions, which, I propose, are interdependent. In many instances, the failure of previous attempts to address the problem stems not from the solutions proposed but from their partial rather than their complete implementation (*Access to Justice*, Interim Report of Lord Woolf, 1995, London).

In the system that Lord Woolf examined, the main responsibility for the initiation and conduct of proceedings rested with the parties to each individual case, and it was normally the plaintiff (now claimant) who set the pace. Thus, Lord Woolf also noted:

Without effective judicial control, the adversarial process is likely to encourage an adversarial culture and to degenerate into an environment in which the litigation process is too often seen as a battlefield where no rules apply. In this environment, questions of expense, delay, compromise and fairness have only a low priority. The consequence is that the expense is often excessive, disproportionate and unpredictable; and delay is frequently unreasonable.

The new civil process

The Civil Procedure Rules 1998 (CPR) apply to both the county court and the High Court. They apply to all cases except (Pt 2) to insolvency proceedings, family proceedings and non-contentious probate proceedings. The vocabulary will be more user-friendly, so, for example, what used to be called a 'writ' is now a 'claim form' and a *guardian ad litem* is a 'litigator's friend'.

Although, in some ways, all the fuss about the CPR being so far reaching creates the impression that the future will see a sharp rise in litigation, the truth may be different. It seems likely that a fall off in litigation in the 1990s will continue. In the Queen's Bench Division, the total number of claims and originating summonses issued fell by 63% to 26,876. 52% of court judgments related to personal injury cases, 65% were for sums in excess of £50,000. In the county court, the number of claims fell by just over 6%.

The overriding objective

The overriding objective of the Civil Procedure Rules (CPR) is to enable the court to deal justly with cases. The first rule reads:

> 1.1(1) These rules are a new procedural code with the overriding objective of enabling the court to deal with cases justly.

This objective includes ensuring that the parties are on an equal footing, and saving expense. When exercising any discretion given by the CPR, the court must, according to r 1.2, have regard to the overriding objective, and a checklist of factors, including the amount of money involved, the complexity of the issue, the parties' financial positions, how the case can be dealt with expeditiously and by allotting an appropriate share of the court's resources while taking into account the needs of others.

Following the Civil Procedure Act 1997, the changes are effected through the new Civil Procedure Rules 1998. These have been supplemented by new practice directions and pre-action protocols. The principal parts of all of these new rules and guidelines are examined below. Thus, 'r 4.1' refers to r 4.1 of the Civil Procedure Rules.

There are three main aspects to the reforms:

(1) Judicial case management

The judge is a case manager in the new regime. He or she is centre stage for the whole action. Previously, lawyers from either side were permitted to wrangle almost endlessly with each other about who should disclose what information and documents to whom and at what stage. Now, the judge is under an obligation to 'actively' manage cases. This includes:

- encouraging parties to co-operate with each other;

- identifying issues in the dispute at an early stage;

- disposing of summary issues which do not need full investigation;

- helping the parties to settle the whole or part of the case;

- fixing timetables for the case hearing and controlling the progress of the case;

- considering whether the benefits of a particular way of hearing the dispute justify its costs.

If the parties refuse to comply with the rules, the practice directions or the protocols, the judge can exercise disciplinary powers. These include:

- using 'Orders for Costs' against parties (that is, refusing to allow the lawyers who have violated the rules to recover their costs from their client or the other side of the dispute);

- 'unless' orders;

- striking-out;

- refusal to grant extensions of time;

- refusal to allow documents not previously disclosed to the court and the other side to be relied upon.

One of the greatest changes, however, concerns the spirit of the law. The new style of procedure which is intended to be brisk will be of paramount importance. The courts will become allergic to delay or any of the old, ponderous, long-winded techniques previously used by many lawyers.

(2)   Pre-action protocols

Part of the problem in the past has arisen from the fact that the courts can only start to exercise control over the progress of a case, and the way it is handled, once proceedings have been issued. Before that stage, lawyers were at liberty to take inordinate time to do things related to the case, to write to lawyers on the other side to the dispute and so forth. Now, a mechanism allows new pre-action requirements to be enforced. Two protocols have been drawn up, to apply in the largest areas of litigation: clinical negligence (including actions against doctors, nurses, dentists, hospitals, health authorities, etc); and personal injury (road accidents, work accidents, etc).

The objects of the protocols are:

- to encourage greater contact between the parties at the earliest opportunity;

- to encourage a better exchange of information;

- to encourage better pre-action investigation;

- to put parties in a position to settle cases fairly and early; and

- to reduce the need for the case going all the way to court.

(3)   Alternatives to going to court

Rule 4.1 requires the court as a part of its 'active case management' to encourage and facilitate the use of alternative dispute resolution (ADR), and r 26.4 allows the court to stay proceedings (that is, halt them) to allow the parties to go to ADR either where the parties themselves request it or where the court 'of its own initiative' considers it appropriate.

At the heart of the new system is the allocation of cases to a 'track' according to their complexity and value.

The small claims track

There is no longer any 'automatic reference' to the small claims track. Claims are allocated to this track in exactly the same way as to the fast or multi-tracks. The concept of an *arbitration*, therefore, disappears and is replaced by a *small claims hearing*. Aspects of the old small claims procedure which are retained include their informality, the interventionist approach adopted by the judiciary, the limited costs regime and the limited grounds for appeal (misconduct of the district judge or an error of law made by the court).

Changes to the handling of small claims are:

* *jurisdiction of up to £5,000* (with the exception of claims for personal injury where the damages sought must be no more than £ 1,000 and for housing disrepair where the claim for repairs and other work and any other claim for damages are both under £ 1,000);

* *paper adjudication, if parties consent* – where a judge thinks that paper adjudication may be appropriate, parties will be asked to say whether or not they have any objections within a given time period. If a party does object, the matter will be given a hearing in the normal way;

- *parties need not attend the hearing* – a party not wishing to attend a hearing will be able to give the court and the other party, or parties, written notice that they will not be attending. The notice must be filed with the court seven days before the start of the hearing. This will guarantee that the court will take into account any written evidence that party has sent to the court. A consequence of this is that the judge must give reasons for the decision reached which will be included in the judgment;

- *the introduction of tailored directions* – to be given for some of the most common small claims, for example, spoiled holidays, or wedding videos, road traffic accidents, building disputes.

Parties can consent to use the small claims track even if the value of their claim exceeds the normal value for that track, but subject to the court's approval. The limited cost regime will not apply to these claims. But costs will be limited to the costs that might have been awarded if the claim had been dealt with in the fast track. Parties will also be restricted to a maximum one day hearing.

The fast track

In accordance with one of the main principles of the Woolf reforms, the purpose of the fast track is to provide a streamlined procedure for the handling of moderately-valued cases – *those with a value of more than £5,000 but less than £15,000* – in a way which will ensure that the costs remain proportionate to the amount in dispute. The features of the procedure which aim to achieve this are:

- standard directions for trial preparation which avoid complex procedures and multiple experts, with minimum case management intervention by the court;

- a limited period between directions and the start of the trial, or trial period, of around 30 weeks;

- a maximum of one day (five hours) for trial;

- trial period must not exceed three weeks and parties must be given 21 days' notice of the date fixed for trial;

- normally, no oral expert evidence to be given at trial; and fixed costs allowed for the trial which vary depending on the level of advocate.

Directions given to the parties by the judge will normally include a date by which parties must file a listing questionnaire. As with allocation questionnaires, the procedural judge may impose a sanction where a listing questionnaire is not returned by the due date. Listing questionnaires will include information about witnesses, confirm the time needed for trial, parties' availability and the level of advocate for the trial.

The multi-track

The multi-track is intended to provide a flexible regime for the handling of the higher value, more complex claims, that is, those with a *value of over £15,000.*

This track does not provide any standard procedure, such as those for small claims or claims in the fast track. Instead, it offers a range of case management tools – *standard directions, case management conferences and pre trial reviews* – which can be used in a 'mix and match' way to suit the needs of individual cases. Whichever of these is used to manage the case, the principle of setting a date for trial, or a trial period at the earliest possible time, no matter that it is some way away, will remain paramount.

Where a trial period is given for a multi-track case, this will be one week. Parties will be told initially that their trial will begin on a day within the given week. The rules and practice direction do not set any time period for giving notice to the parties of the date fixed for trial.

Experts

New rules place a clear duty on the court to ensure that 'expert evidence is restricted to that which is reasonably required to resolve the proceedings'. That is to say, expert evidence is only allowed either by way of written report, or orally, where the court gives permission. Equally important is the rules' statement about experts' duties. They state that it is the clear duty of experts to help the *court* on matters within their expertise, bearing in mind that this duty overrides any obligation to the person from whom they have received instructions or by whom they are paid.

There will be greater emphasis in the future on using the opinion of a single expert. Experts are only called to give oral evidence at a trial or hearing if the court gives permission. Experts' written reports must contain a statement that they understand and have complied with their duty to the court. Instructions to experts are no longer be privileged and their substance, whether written or oral, must be set out in the expert's report. Thus, either side can insist, through the court, on seeing how the other side phrased its request to an expert.

Criticism of the new reforms

Professor Michael Zander QC has made substantial criticism of the new civil procedure reforms.

At the heart of the Woolf reforms is the mechanism of 'judicial case management'. Looking at the results of an

American study about how the system operates in the United States, Zander raises serious questions about whether the Woolf reforms would be subject to similar problems.

The major official study that Zander examined was published by the Institute of Civil Justice at the Rand Corporation in California. The study was based on 10,000 cases in Federal Courts drawn from 16 States. It appears that a range of judicial case management techniques introduced in America had little effect on the time it took to deal with cases, litigation costs and lawyer satisfaction. There was evidence that early judicial case management is associated with significantly increased costs to litigants because lawyer work increases in such circumstances.

The Rand Report explains that case management tends to increase rather than reduce costs because it generates more work by lawyer. Zander notes that lawyer work may increase as a result of earlier management because lawyers need to respond to a court's management; for example, talking to the litigant and to the other lawyers in advance of a conference with the judge, travelling and spending time at the court house, meeting with the judge and updating the file after conference.

Professor Zander has taken the view that the reasons for delay in civil legal process are not primarily to do with the adversarial nature of civil litigation. The only serious empirical study of the reasons for delay, argues Zander, is that done by KPMG Peat Marwick for the Lord Chancellor's Department in 1994. The KPMG report identified seven causes of delay:

- the nature of the case;

- delay caused by the parties;

- delay caused by their representatives;

- external factors, such as the difficulty of getting experts' reports;

- the judiciary;

- court procedures; and

- court administration.

How the lawyers play the adversary game was not one of these factors. KPMG considered the relative important of the seven factors and found that the two factors that gave rise to the most significant delay were, first, delay caused by lawyers, mainly due to pressure of work and inexperience or inefficiency in the handling of the case by the parties' solicitors and, secondly, the time taken to obtain medical or other expert reports.

The new civil process

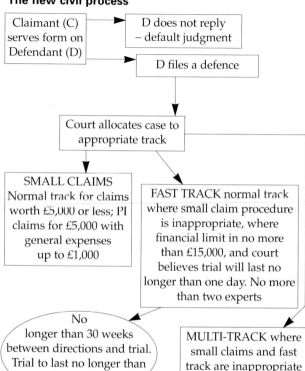

Claimant (C) serves form on Defendant (D) → D does not reply – default judgment

→ D files a defence

↓

Court allocates case to appropriate track

SMALL CLAIMS
Normal track for claims worth £5,000 or less; PI claims for £5,000 with general expenses up to £1,000

FAST TRACK normal track where small claim procedure is inappropriate, where financial limit in no more than £15,000, and court believes trial will last no longer than one day. No more than two experts

No longer than 30 weeks between directions and trial. Trial to last no longer than three weeks

MULTI-TRACK where small claims and fast track are inappropriate

Case management conference
used for judge to control timetable, clearly define issues, and resolve how expert evidence and disclosure to be dealt with

6 Tribunals, inquiries and arbitration

Reasons for their creation

There has grown up over the years a network of administrative tribunals dealing with specific areas of specialism. This has been the consequence of increased State interference into social and economic fields.

Because of the technical and specialised nature of these disputes it is thought that the ordinary courts are ill-equipped to deal with them. The procedure of the ordinary courts is slow and administrative decisions need to be made quickly for efficiency. Delay can cause a claimant severe financial hardship in some cases, and therefore tribunals are favoured over the formal procedures of the courts which are often very expensive.

Administrative tribunals

The workload of the courts is relieved by a large number of administrative tribunals. Tribunals deal with a wide area:

and many more. As society has progressed, certain areas have developed in which complicated disputes concerning technical matters can arise. These disputes are more often than not between private individuals and government departments, hence the term 'administrative tribunals'.

The Tribunals and Inquiries Acts

Tribunals and Inquiries Acts 1958; 1971; 1992.

The Council on Tribunals was established in 1958 and provides general guidance to administrative tribunals. Members are appointed by the Lord Chancellor.

Composition of tribunals

Tribunals normally consist of a panel of lay members with a chairman who has some legal knowledge. Lack of legal knowledge is not viewed as a drawback, because what is necessary is a cheap, swift, informal method of resolving disputes, and in technical areas cases heard by an expert in that field is more desirable than legal knowledge.

Under the Trade Union Reform and Employment Rights Act 1993, the tribunal chairman will be able to sit alone to hear certain types of cases.

Statutory tribunals

Social security/welfare

An individual has a right to appeal to the Social Security Appeal Tribunal if their application is rejected. The tribunal consists of three members, a chairman who is legally trained, and two lay members. Further appeal lies to the Social Security Commissioners, and further to the Court of Appeal on a question of law.

Tribunals dealing with revenue
These tribunals hear appeals against taxation and VAT assessments. A recently established tribunal, the Valuation and Council Tax Tribunal, deals with appeals against the council tax.

Lands tribunals
There are a number of tribunals which deal with issues relating to land, for example, against compulsory purchase. The lands tribunal is an important tribunal with status similar to the High Court.

Tribunals dealing with transportation
The transport tribunal deals with issues such as appeals over road haulage licences.

Employment tribunals
The main role of these tribunals is to deal with issues relating to employment, for example, discrimination in employment, unfair dismissal, redundancy claims and issues related to health and safety at work. The Industrial Tribunals Act 1996 has consolidated the existing primary legislation in this area.

Mental health review tribunals
These tribunals generally consist of members of the medical profession deciding issues related to matters under the Mental Health Act 1983.

Immigration appeal tribunals
This body hears appeals from individuals who are refused entry into the UK or refused permission to extend their stay. Its work is often politically sensitive, particularly given the current world situation and the restrictions on judicial review imposed by the Anti-terrorism, Crime and Security Act 2001.

INFORMALITY:
tribunals are less
formal than
courts; no formal
rule of evidence

SPEED:
tribunals operate
more quickly
than the ordinary
courts

**ADVANTAGES
OF
TRIBUNALS**

FLEXIBILITY:
more flexible
than courts; not
contained by
rules of
precedent; have
a wide discretion

COST:
cheaper than
ordinary courts;
costs not
normally
awarded

SPECIALISM:
operate in
specialised fields;
possess expertise
in specific fields

Lack of
representation

Hearings in
private

Appeals provisions
inadequate

**DISADVANTAGES OF
TRIBUNALS**

No adherence to
precedent

Members could
be biased

Expediency at
the expense of
justice

Domestic tribunals

These relate to matters of private rather than public concern and can be set up by legalisation. Examples of domestic tribunals are committees established to discipline their members, for example, barristers are subject to the control of their Inns of Court and the Senate of the Inns of Court and the Bar.

Other professions come under similar scrutiny by their controlling body. These tribunals possess tremendous powers. Where the tribunal has been set up by statute, judicial review will usually lie. In other cases it will depend on the willingness of the courts to get involved. The courts must apply the principles of natural justice to ensure the tribunal has not acted *ultra vires* (*Lee v Showmen's Guild of Great Britain* (1952)).

Control of tribunals

By the courts

Courts can exercise some control over tribunals. There is normally a provision for a right to appeal on a point of law to the ordinary courts. The courts can further exercise controls over tribunals by the use of 'prerogative' orders in judicial review proceedings, to ensure tribunals apply the rules of natural justice.

Control by the Council on Tribunals

This is a permanent body of up to 15 members appointed by the Lord Chancellor to review the constitution and working of administrative tribunals, and to examine rules of procedure.

The Ombudsman

An official appointed by Parliament to hear complaints from individuals who have suffered administrative mismanagement. The Ombudsman system has been introduced into banking and insurance. Under s 21 of the Courts and Legal Services Act 1990, a Legal Service Ombudsman has been appointed by the Lord Chancellor to investigate complaints about professional bodies in the legal profession, for example, licensed conveyances.

Courts with special jurisdiction

Restrictive Practices Court;

Coroners Court;

Courts Martial; and

Ecclesiastical Courts.

Future and control of the tribunal system

It is argued that control and supervision of the system cannot rest with one body alone – the Council of Tribunals. The courts do exercise some control through appeal or review, but it is stated that there needs to be a uniform code of procedure to govern the workings of tribunals which would promote more safeguards and consistency. Questions posed are:

- should the Council on Tribunals be given extended powers?;

- should its composition be altered and its resources increased?;

- should it be afforded a political base in the form of a select committee in Parliament?

Various reports have drawn attention to issues concerning the tribunal system:

- the Special Report of the Council in 1980, *The Functions of the Council on Tribunals* (Cmnd 7805); and

- the JUSTICE/All Souls Report, *Administrative Justice* (1988).

Inquiries

Inquiries are usually established on an *ad hoc* basis when it is necessary to deal with a specific issue, for example:

- to investigate major accidents by air, sea or rail;

- to investigate companies under the Companies Act; and

- inquiries into a specific event.

Arbitration

Arbitration is a means of settling disputes other than by court action and arises when one or more persons are appointed to hear the arguments put forward by the parties and to decide upon them.

Advantages of arbitration

- A matter can be referred to arbitration by the court.

- A court may refer a matter to arbitration by Acts of Parliament or by agreement, if the issues concerned are complex and technical.

- Agreement can be in any form, oral or written, but the Arbitration Act only applies to agreements in writing.

- The agreement normally names the arbitrator, but the agreement can specify a specific body, for example, a trade or profession.

- The arbitrator can examine witnesses and parties concerned on oath, and require parties to submit documents, accounts, etc.

- The arbitrator makes an award, this is final – no rights of appeal, the arbitrator can order the party to pay the entire costs of the proceedings if they lose.

- Where there is an arbitration agreement and one party nevertheless brings court proceedings on the application of the other party, the court will 'stay' proceedings.

- The arbitration agreement must cover the dispute which is before the court, otherwise the court will not stay proceedings.

- The person asking for the stay must have taken no part in the court proceedings.

Procedure in arbitration

Duty of arbitrator

The duty of the arbitrator is to resolve the dispute by making an award. The arbitrator can employ a legal adviser if necessary to help him draw up the award if he feels he is not competent to deal with the legal issues involved. The arbitrator fixes the time and place for hearing the parties and will inform them of this arrangement. If the arbitrator has specialised technical knowledge, he can dispense with the need for expert witnesses. This reduces costs.

If an important point of law arises, the arbitrator can 'state a case' for the opinion of the court. When the opinion of the court is given, the arbitrator applies the law to the facts of the case and makes his award. The arbitrator can decide that it is not necessary to 'state a case'. He can, however, be compelled to do this by one of the parties.

The award is final. However, the court can set aside an award on procedural grounds if:

Arbitrator has misconducted himself, or award obtained by improper means	Arbitrator refuses to hear one of the parties
Witnesses were examined in the absence of one of the parties	Arbitrator has been in communication with one of the parties about the issues involved

Enforcement

The party in whose favour the award has been made can enforce the award in the same way as he could a court judgment.

The Arbitration Act 1996 provides that the object of arbitration is the fair resolution of disputes by an impartial tribunal without unnecessary delay or expense. It says that the parties should be free to agree how their disputes are resolved, subject only to such safeguards as are necessary in the public interest. Courts can only intervene as far as the Act allows them to do so. In order to be governed by the Act, arbitration agreements must be made in writing. Under the Act, a party is entitled to appeal to a law court to challenge the award made in arbitral proceedings on the ground of a 'serious irregularity' affecting the tribunal, the proceedings or the award. Nonetheless, the Act greatly restricts the scope of appeals that may be made to a law court on a point of law.

Mediation

Mediation is the process whereby a third party acts as the medium through which two disputing parties can communicate and negotiate in order to resolve a problem without recourse to the courts. It is most commonly used in divorce matters. Mediation was particularly emphasised in the Family Law Act 1996. However, Lord Irvine (the Lord Chancellor) announced in 1999 that the proposals in the 1996 Act would not be implemented in 2000 as intended, because of the extent of the criticism from legal practitioners and academics. This did not signal the end of mediation altogether, but its scope is undoubtedly narrower than Parliament had intended in 1996.

7 The jury system

The role of the jury

TO DECIDE THE FACTS OF THE CASE

They are lay persons, they have no knowledge of law and are not competent to put forward any opinion on law. They rely on their common sense to assess the accused and the evidence against him in order to reach a verdict. If the verdict is an acquittal, it is unchallengeable.

FUNCTION OF THE JUDGE

Inter alia, to explain the law to the jury so it can reach a verdict. At the conclusion of the evidence, to sum up the case before the jury retires to reach a verdict. The judge has no judicial power to instruct a jury to convict an accused: *DPP v Stonehouse* (1978).

- Once the accused is acquitted, he cannot be charged with the same offence again. This has been much criticised, most recently in the Macpherson Report (1999).

  However, Baldwin and McConville in *Jury Trials* (1979) established no evidence to suggest that juries acquitted people in the face of unjust prosecution.

- Section 36 of the Criminal Justice Act 1972 does provide for a procedure whereby points of law which arise in a criminal case where the defendant has been acquitted, can be referred to the Court of Appeal by the Attorney General to see if any loopholes in the law can be amended. This does not, however, affect the original verdict.

ELIGIBILITY

Juries Act 1974 lays down the rules for selecting a jury

Criminal Justice Act 1987 allows as of right excusal to those over 65

Anyone listed on the electoral register between the ages of 18 and 70 resident in the UK for at least five years since the age of 13

Members of the judiciary

Barristers, solicitors

INELIGIBLE

The clergy

The mentally ill

The Criminal Justice and Public Order Act 1994 has disqualified people on bail from sitting on a jury.

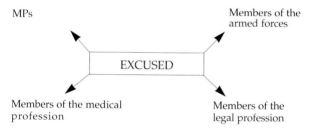

MPs

Members of the armed forces

EXCUSED

Members of the medical profession

Members of the legal profession

Selection of the jury

Those entitled to be excused by administrative discretion:

- any person who has served on a jury in the last two years;

- persons with good reason to be excused (s 120 of the Criminal Justice Act 1988).

Challenging jury membership

Jury membership may be challenged if:

- the juror is in fact not qualified; or

- the juror is biased; or

- the juror may be reasonably suspected of bias against the defendant (s 12(4)).

Juries Act 1974
The prosecution has a right to challenge as well as the defence, and also has the right to ask a juror to 'stand by' for the Crown.

The Attorney General has laid down guidelines as to when the prosecution can exercise the right:

- if a jury check shows information to support exercising the right to stand by; or

- if the person to be sworn in as a juror is unsuitable and the defence agree (*Practice Note* (1988)).

Either side can challenge the array.

Peremptory challenge
In the past, the defence had the right of peremptory challenge, whereby it could challenge up to three jurors without giving any reasons. The right to peremptory challenge was abolished by the Criminal Justice Act 1988 (s 118).

Jury vetting

The panel is selected at random, and any party to the proceedings can inspect the panel from which the jurors will be chosen.

Jury vetting is the investigation of jurors' backgrounds to determine whether they are suitable for jury service.

The practice first came to public notice in 1978 during the 'ABC trial', a case brought under the Official Secrets Act 1911.

Two cases in 1980 highlighted the practice of jury 'settling': *Crown Court at Sheffield ex p Brownlow* (1980); *Mason* (1980).

Challenging jury membership

Jury membership can be challenged if:

- Juror is not qualified
- Juror is biased
- Suspicion juror may be biased

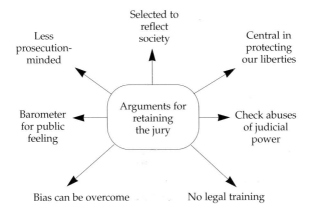

Selected to reflect society

Less prosecution-minded

Central in protecting our liberties

Barometer for public feeling

Arguments for retaining the jury

Check abuses of judicial power

Bias can be overcome

No legal training

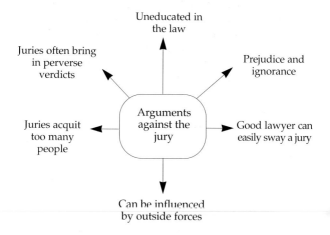

Uneducated in the law

Juries often bring in perverse verdicts

Prejudice and ignorance

Arguments against the jury

Juries acquit too many people

Good lawyer can easily sway a jury

Can be influenced by outside forces

The constitutional position of this practice is much in doubt and has been criticised. However, the legitimacy and that of the Crown's right to 'stand by' potential jurors is clearly stated by the Court of Appeal in *Bettaney* (1985). The Attorney General issued a Practice Note in 1988 and also issued a statement confirming the previous guidelines.

Changes to the jury system

The jury is thought to be one of the most vital features of the English legal system and a fundamental safeguard to our liberty. However, the jury has been criticised over the years.

The most influential of the recent studies is Penny Darbyshire's 'The lamp that shows that freedom lives – is it worth a candle?', which was produced as a result of her experience of serving on a jury. Her aim was:

… to question the traditional qualifications used in praise and defence of the jury, suggesting that some of them are conceptually unsound … [to] argue that jury defenders inflate the jury's importance by portraying the 'right' to jury trial as central to the criminal justice system and as a guardian of due process and civil liberties.

Darbyshire criticises the traditional view of the jury and criticises those commentators who emphasise the 'mystery' of the jury. Juries, she states, are not a representative sample of the population. She points out that they are:

An antidemocratic, irrational and haphazard legislator, whose erratic and secret decisions run counter to the rule of the law.

The Royal Commission on Criminal Justice has put forward proposals to reduce the role of the jury in criminal trials.

Although the jury is seen to be an important cornerstone of the English legal system, few in-depth studies have been made of it. Some commentators have tended to view the jury in a romantic light, which, it is argued, is detrimental to change in the justice system.

Darbyshire's arguments tend to imply that it plays such a small role in the minority of cases, its passing would not be cause for lament.

Others argue, however, that the jury system performs a very important service and it should be protected at all costs.

The use of the jury in English law dates back into history. However, today, the use of juries has declined:

- The Administration of Justice Act 1933 limited the use of juries in civil cases.

- In 1986, the Roskill Report advocated the abolition of a right to jury trial in complex fraud cases.

- Lord Denning has argued that some jurors are not adequately suited to the task required of them.

- Reforms to the Criminal Damage Act 1971 have taken certain cases away from the jury, making them summary offences.

- Part V of the Criminal Justice Act 1988 removed the right to jury trial in other offences including driving whilst disqualified.

- In its study, *The Distribution of Criminal Business between the Crown Court and Magistrates' Courts* (1975), the James Committee recommended that minor thefts and similar offences should become summary offences.

- In civil cases, the use of the jury has almost disappeared and the Coroner's Court has been modified by the Criminal Law Act 1977.

- The Northern Ireland (Emergency Provisions) Act 1991 has taken away the right to jury trial for defendants in serious criminal cases.

- It is possible for a judge to curtail the jury by asking for a special verdict: *Bourne* (1952); *Robbins* (1988).

Some commentators have argued for reform of the jury along the lines of continental procedures. The Royal Commission (*Runciman Commission*) conducted a study of pre-trial procedures used in France and Germany (Leigh and Zedner, *A Report on the Administration of Criminal Justice in the Pretrial Phase in France and Germany* (1992)), although this has not gained favour.

Reform of the jury system

The 1999 jury proposals

In 1999, the government announced its intention to introduce legislation to curb the right to jury trial. In essence, it wishes, in cases triable either-way, to disallow a defendant from insisting upon trial by jury in circumstances where magistrates believe that they are well suited to hear the case. More than 18,500 defendants a year would lose their right to trial by jury under these plans. The plans were advanced by the government to, according to its own contentions, speed up the hearing of criminal cases. The proposed reform was widely condemned by civil rights groups, the Bar and other lawyers.

The government decided to push ahead with the change after finding that many people who opt in the early stages of their cases for trial by jury change their plea to guilty before the trial is heard. Home Office research shows that more than 70% of those who opt for jury trial plead guilty by the day their Crown Court case opens. The average cost of a jury trial is £13,500, compared with £2,500 for a hearing by magistrates.

In order to research the matter further, and as part of a review of the whole criminal justice system, the government commissioned the Auld Report. It was published in September 2001, and its main recommendations on the jury system were:

- jurors should be more widely representative than they are of the national and local communities from which they are drawn. Except for those with criminal convictions or mental disorder, no one in future should be ineligible for or excusable as of right from jury service;

- the law should not be extended to permit more intrusive research than is already possible into the workings of juries. The law should be declared, by statute if need be, that juries have no right to acquit defendants in defiance of the law or in disregard of the evidence;

- the defendant should no longer have an elective right to trial by jury in 'either-way' cases.

These recommendations may be put forward by the government in 2002, but they will face fierce opposition from the House of Lords. In a previous Bill the government failed to get provisions which restricted the right to trial by jury through the House of Lords stage. The proposals also face significant opposition from lawyers and civil liberties groups.

8   Access to justice

The Access to Justice Act 1999 introduced a new structure to help people who cannot otherwise afford to use lawyers to do so. It introduces the Legal Services Commission (LSC) to replace the Legal Aid Board, and the Community Legal Service (CLS) to organise the provision of free legal services locally. The Act also introduces the Criminal Defence Service (CDS) to provide lawyers to people without sufficient means who need defence lawyers in criminal cases.

The history of legal aid

Legal aid was not available until after the Second World War; prior to that, individuals needing legal advice had to depend on the generosity of lawyers taking their case for a bare fee.

In 1903, the Poor Prisoners' Defence Act provided, for the first time, that lawyers were to be paid from public funds.

The State system of legal aid was created through a series of statutes:

- Legal Aid Acts 1949 and 1964;

- Criminal Justice Act 1967;

- Legal Advice and Assistance Act 1972;

- Legal Aid Act 1974;

- Legal Aid Act 1979 (as amended 1985);

- Legal Aid Act 1988.

Reasons for increases in legal aid

The number of recorded crimes has risen from around 1% in the 1950s to 4% in 1989. With this increased crime rate and police involvement in the criminal courts, the increase in legal costs has been inevitable.

Eligibility for legal aid

Eligibility for legal aid is dependent on the individual's financial circumstances.

Legal aid limits were set at the same level as supplementary benefits in 1974 and increased each year as a result. The Murphy Report concluded that, since 1979, more than 10 million people have lost their eligibility for civil legal aid on the basis of income.

The Legal Aid Act 1988

Until 1999, the legal aid scheme and the Legal Aid Board were governed by the Legal Aid Act 1988. This Act has now been repealed, and 'legal aid' in its original form no longer exists.

The Community Legal Service

Until recently, about £800 million a year was spent on lawyers' fees under the civil legal aid system. Another £150 million a year from local government, central government, charities and businesses is spent on the voluntary advice sector, including Citizens' Advice Bureaux, law centres and other advice centres. The Legal Services Commission (replacing the Legal Aid Board) was intended to take the lead in establishing a Community Legal Service, co-ordinating the provision of legal services in every region. The LSC manages the CLS fund, which has replaced legal aid in civil and family cases.

The reasons for change

The main reasons that the government decided a change was necessary were as follows:

- The system was too heavily biased towards expensive court based solutions to people's problems.

- Despite a merits test, legal aid was sometimes used to fund cases that appear to be undeserving.

- It was not possible to control spending effectively. From 1992–93 to 1997–98, spending on civil and family legal aid grew by 35% from £586 million to £793 million; but, at the same time, the number of cases funded actually fell by 31% from 419,861 to 319,432.

- In the ordinary legal aid system, lawyers were paid according to the amount of work claimed for, so there is no incentive to handle cases quickly or work efficiently.

How the new system works

The Legal Services Commission buys services for the public under contracts. Only lawyers and other providers with contracts are able to work under the new scheme. This enables budgets to be strictly controlled, helps to endure quality of service, and provides a basis for competition between providers. The fund is targeted towards those people who are most in need of help, and high priority cases. There is no absolute entitlement to help, and the fund is not spent on cases which could be financed by other means, such as conditional fee arrangements ('no win, no fee'). Also, those who can afford to contribute towards their legal expenses are required to do so. The government has been encouraging a widening of legal insurance cover and conditional fees for those people who are not eligible for funding.

The Access to Justice Act 1999

Under the new system, legal aid is no longer available for:

- those seeking accident compensation (except clinical negligence cases);

- disputes about inheritance under a will or an intestacy;

- matters affecting the administration of a trust or the position of a trustee;

- matters relating to the position of directors of companies, restoring a company to the Register or dealing with the position of minority shareholders;

- matters affecting partnerships;

- matters before the Lands Tribunal;

- cases between landowners over a disputed boundary of adjacent property; and

- cases pursued in the course of a business.

The hope is that the extension of conditional fees in these areas will provide increased public access to lawyers.

The government has said it is committed to:

(1) allowing conditional fee agreements (no win, no fee agreements) to be used in all except family and criminal cases;

(2) transferring to conditional fees most money and damages claims previously supported by legal aid;

(3) removing most personal injury actions from the scope of legal aid;

(4) ensuring that clinical negligence cases to be conducted only by practitioners who are experienced in this field of litigation;

(5) the setting up of a limited transitional fund which would provide support in cases where there are high investigative costs in establishing the merits of a case or where the costs of carrying the case are very high.

The 1999 Act introduced new financial conditions on the grant of public funding for civil claims:

- Services will be provided in some cases subject to the assisted person agreeing to repay an amount in excess of the cost of the services provided in the event that their case is successful.

- It is now possible to require the assisted person to repay, over time and with interest, the full cost of the service provided. Thus, in some cases, the provision of services will take the form of a loan scheme.

The Conditional Fees Order 1998

The right to use 'no win, no fee' agreements to pursue civil law claims was extended by the Conditional Fees Order 1998. The order allows lawyers to offer conditional fee agreements to their clients in all civil cases excluding family cases.

With the introduction of companies such as 'Claims Direct' and 'The Accident Group', the last few years have seen a significant increase in the number of people taking advantage of conditional fee arrangements (CFAs) to bring personal injury claims. The government has noted that many of these people would have been unable to afford to pursue their claims at all without conditional fees – people who are only just above the legal aid/CLS limit, and are far from well off.

The Access to Justice Act 1999 reformed the law relating to conditional fees. It enables the court to order the losing party to pay, in addition to the other party's normal legal costs, the uplift on the successful party's lawyers' fees. Also, in any case where a litigant has insured facing an order for the other side's costs, the losing party may be ordered to cover the premium paid by the successful party for that insurance.

Clinical negligence cases

Funding has been retained for clinical negligence cases because conditional fee arrangements are much more difficult to come by than in other personal injury claims. It is a very specialist area of litigation, and it can be difficult to identify at the outset whether a case has merit, and even as the case unfolds whether the alleged negligence has caused the ailment or injury. The Lord Chancellor stated in 1999 that lawyers needed time to modernise their firms in such a way as to make them able to take on clinical negligence claims regardless of the means of the claimant. The legal profession has, over the past few years, become more and more specialised, and there are now firms of solicitors and individual barristers who have considerable expertise in the area.

Levels of funding

There are two broad categories of funding in civil cases: 'Initial Legal Help' and 'Higher levels of funding'. Initial Legal Help covers the cost of getting advice from a solicitor. It is available to those whose disposable income is no more than £87 per week, and their disposable capital is no more than £1,000. More funding may be available if, for instance, the case is going to court. This will depend on the chances of the case succeeding and the means of the applicant. The means limits for the higher levels of funding are higher than for Initial Legal Help. In 2000–01, a total of 108,013 bills were paid by the CLS in non-family civil cases. The total cost was £527 million, the average cost of each case being £4,876.

Criminal Defence Service

The Criminal Defence Service (CDS) replaced the old system of criminal legal aid on 2 April 2001. The Access to Justice Act 1999 states that the CDS was created:

> For the purpose of securing that individuals involved in criminal investigations or criminal proceedings have access to such advice, assistance and representation as the interests of justice require.

The CDS is run by the Legal Services Commission, but it is an entirely separate scheme from the Community Legal Service, with a separate budget. The Commission enters into contracts with legal service providers for different types of criminal defence services. All contracts include quality requirements and prices are usually fixed in advance. Fixed prices provide an incentive to avoid delay, and reward efficient practice. Opponents of the system, however, have argued that fixed-price work is not conducive to justice, and encourages corner-cutting. If a case requires the services of a specialist advocate in the Crown Court, this is usually covered by a separate contract.

Very complex and expensive cases – where the trial is expected to last 25 days or more – are not covered by ordinary contracts. A defendant's choice of solicitor is limited to firms on a specialist panel, and a separate contract will be agreed in each case.

As of 2 April 2001, solicitors in private practice can only carry out criminal defence work for the CDS if they have a 'General Criminal Contract' (GCC). Firms can apply for a crime category franchise, and will be awarded one if they pass an audit by the Legal Services Commission. There are three types of GCC: the 'All Classes' contract, the Prison Law contract and the Criminal Cases Review Commission contract.

There are six pilot schemes currently in place to assess the possibility of a Public Defender Service, which would be a salaried defence service for defenders employed with the CDS. Some lawyers have expressed fear at this proposal. The Law Society is concerned that famous campaigning lawyers such as Gareth Peirce (who helped release the Guildford Four and the Birmingham Six) and Jim Nicol (who represented the appellants in the Carl Bridgewater case) might be shunned by the CDS.

There are two ways in which an individual can be helped by the CDS: 'Advice and Assistance', and 'Representation'.

Advice and Assistance

Advice and Assistance covers help from a solicitor, including giving general advice, writing letters, negotiating, getting a barrister's opinion and preparing a written case. It is means tested, and the current level under which a person will qualify is £87 per week in disposable income, and £1,000 in disposable capital. In some instances separate 'Advocacy Assistance' will be appropriate. This covers the cost of a solicitor preparing a case and initial representation in the magistrates' or the Crown Court. It also covers representation in some prison law cases.

Representation

Representation is available for those charged with a criminal offence, and is granted by application to the magistrates' court. It covers the cost of a solicitor to prepare a defence before going to court, and to provide representation. It may also be available for bail applications. If the case requires a barrister, then those fees are also covered. It can also cover advice on appeal against verdict or sentence. Representation will be granted where it is 'in the interests of justice'. It will usually be in the interests of justice to grant representation where a custodial sentence is likely, or where there are substantial questions of law to be argued. The defendant may be asked to contribute to the costs where it is reasonable for them to do so.

Duty solicitor schemes

Duty solicitor schemes operate in police stations, and the magistrates' and Crown Courts. The solicitor on duty is there to give legal advice to those who require it quickly, and without means testing.

Alternative legal services

• Legal Advice Centres

    Normally found in Citizen's Advice Bureaux or universities; lawyers give free advice, usually regarding areas of welfare law.

• Citizen's Advice Bureaux

    The workers in the Citizen's Advice Bureau are usually trained in dealing with clients' problems, of which a great number are legally based.

Law centres

These were established in 1968 by the Society of Labour Lawyers in *Justice For All*. They were established to:

- educate the public in their rights and duties under the law; and

- specialise in specific areas of law which were seen as appropriate to poorer sections of the community, such as landlord and tenant, employment law and social security law.